A Teen
Eating Disorder
Prevention
Book

Understanding Bulimia Nervosa

Debbie Stanley

A HAZELDEN/ROSEN BOOK

Published in 1999 by The Rosen Publishing Group, Inc.
29 East 21st Street, New York, NY 10010

Library of Congress Cataloging-in-Publication Data

Stanley, Debbie.
    Understanding Bulimia Nervosa / Debbie Stanley.
        p.   cm. — (A teen eating disorder prevention book)
    Includes bibliographical references and index.
    Summary: Discusses bulimia, an eating disorder which is characterized by alternating episodes of binge eating and purging.
    ISBN 1-56838-261-8
    1. Bulimia Juvenile literature.   2. Eating disorders
Juvenile literature.   [1. Bulimia.   2. Eating disorders.]   I. Title.   II. Series.
    RC552.B84S73   1999
    616.85'263—dc21   99-23311
                                                                    CIP

Manufactured in the United States of America

ABOUT THE AUTHOR

Debbie Stanley has a bachelor's degree in journalism and a master's in industrial/organizational psychology.

To Bethany, the next generation.

Contents

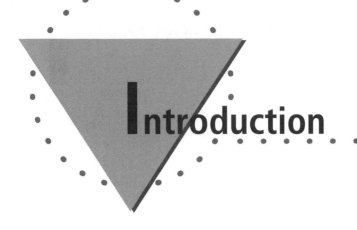

Introduction

Lisa is trying her best to keep up in school, but no matter what she does she can't stay focused. She finds herself daydreaming in class, wondering what life will be like after her parents' divorce is finalized. At night she sometimes has trouble sleeping and wakes up from nightmares. She is sure something is wrong with her because her report cards are never very good and her parents fight over her constantly, plus she doesn't have a boyfriend and all the popular kids ignore her.

Carla is on her school's cheerleading squad. Since she's the smallest, she's usually chosen for the top of the elaborate human pyramids her squad is famous for. Besides cheerleading and keeping up with her schoolwork, Carla also works part-time at a bakery to save up for a car. But despite her busy schedule she always seems to be in a good mood and full of energy.

Scott's goal is to be his school's best varsity wrestler. His dad was an all-star at the same school in his day, and Scott wants to make him proud. He trains hard, making sure he's in perfect shape for each meet, and he takes his dad's advice on what to eat and how to train. Scott is hoping that all of his hard work will pay off with a scholarship to a good university.

An only child, Shauna enjoys reading and doesn't mind being by herself. Her parents, however, are constantly pushing her to put down her books and be more active. Her mother sometimes looks intently at Shauna's waist and tells her she had better stop eating so much, and her father gets angry with her when she can't keep up with him as he hurries across a parking lot or up the stairs at the mall. Most of the time, though, Shauna finds it pretty easy to ignore them since they both work late a lot and she usually has the house to herself.

Kaitlin is a long-distance runner. She enjoys the outdoors and finds that running for miles eases her mind when she has a problem. Her coach encourages her to run as much as she wants, saying that all the extra work will keep her thin and fit and make her an even more important part of the team. Kaitlin sometimes lets her little sister tag along for the first mile when she runs, but most of the time she prefers to go alone.

What is similar about these people? They are of different genders, ages, ethnicities, and social classes. Some are popular in school, and some are not. Some are athletic while others prefer non-physical hobbies. Some are good students, but others struggle to pass each semester. With so many differences, what could they possibly have in common?

It's something no one can see, and even their families and closest friends may be unaware of it, but it rules their lives, invades their thoughts every day, perhaps even every hour, and may eventually kill them. It is an eating disorder called bulimia nervosa, or simply bulimia. Each of these people regularly goes through out-of-control eating sessions called binges, which are followed by desperate attempts to get rid of, or purge, the excess calories.

Lisa's family problems are sabotaging every aspect of her life, but no one is paying enough attention to her to tell her that. She believes that if she could just be good, her parents wouldn't get divorced. Sometimes when she can't sleep or when she wakes up in the middle of the night, Lisa sneaks down to the kitchen and binges on ice cream, chips, cookies, milk, candy bars, and coffee cake. The food doesn't console her, and the empty wrappers and dirty dishes and the painfully full feeling in her stomach all make her realize once again what a failure she is, so she goes to the small bathroom in the basement (where her family can't hear her) and throws it all back up.

At exactly five feet tall, Carla's ideal weight is somewhere around 100 pounds. She enjoys being small because she's always the center of attention in cheerleading—everyone keeps telling her how cute and tiny she is. What no one knows is that over the previous summer, while staying with relatives in another state, Carla got pregnant. She didn't know at first because missing a period was not unusual for her, but when she began to gain weight, she went to a clinic for diet pills. They insisted she have a pregnancy test, then helped her get an abortion. No one, not even her family, knows what happened, but Carla thinks about what happened every day, and when she's feeling really bad she binges, then panics and takes a huge dose of laxatives to keep the food from "sticking."

Scott finds that fasting and exercising for hours on end are the only ways he can drop weight quickly and get into the lowest possible weight class. His dad tells him to drop the weight using tactics he used back when he wrestled. Tricks like exercising in a rubber suit, taking diuretics or "water pills," sitting in a steam room, and not eating for a day or more were once common for wrestlers. Now such practices are recognized as extremely dangerous.

Shauna hates exercise. She feels stupid going outdoors by herself and jumping rope or skating up and down the block, just to please her dad. She has exercise-induced asthma, although she doesn't know it and her parents haven't taken her to a doctor to find out why she has trouble breathing sometimes—they just assume it's laziness. Shauna comes home to a big, empty house after school, and sometimes she's scared to be there by herself. She snacks her way through the same afternoon shows every day, alternating between sweet and salty foods and washing it all down with milk and pop. Sometimes she skips dinner, since she's not really hungry anyway, but sometimes, if she has a bad day at school or if her mother calls and they argue, she gorges her way through every last bit of junk food in the house. By the time she's done she feels so sick she has to throw up. Then she locks herself in her bedroom and climbs into bed with a book.

Kaitlin's running seems healthy to everyone, but it's an example of too much of a good thing. More and more, running has become Kaitlin's one and only coping skill. She runs when she's upset, or sad, or angry, or bored, or unsure of herself. She finds it hard to concentrate on homework if she hasn't run at least four miles. Sometimes she wakes up before the alarm goes off, so she suits up and takes a morning run before getting ready for school. Kaitlin doesn't see anything wrong with it, especially since her coach continues to praise her for working so hard. Plus, she figures it keeps her from gaining weight when she "pigs out" on junk food—something she does a couple of times per week.

These scenarios point out the wide variety of circumstances that, in some people, can lead to bulimia. They also demonstrate how something as serious as bulimia is easily overlooked by parents, coaches, teachers, friends, family members, and even bulimics themselves. This book is intended to help you:

- Learn the facts about bulimia

- Recognize its symptoms and learn to prevent it in yourself and your friends

- Find professional help for yourself or a friend and enlist the aid of parents, teachers, counselors, and coaches in dealing with bulimia and other eating disorders

- Recognize and resist society's unrealistic expectations of physical perfection and refuse to perpetuate them in your evaluation of others

- Develop a positive self-image that includes unconditional acceptance of your physical self

- Begin to evaluate your nutritional habits and fitness level fairly and honestly in order to improve your overall health

Note: Because an estimated 90 to 95 percent of people suffering from bulimia are female, the feminine pronouns ("she" and "her") are used throughout this book instead of "he or she" or "him/her." This is for the sake of clarity and simplicity and is not intended to exclude males, who represent a small but nonetheless real and important segment of bulimics. Boys and young men as well as girls and young women are encouraged to educate themselves on the risk factors and warning signs associated with the disease and to learn how they can help themselves and their friends.

1

Bulimia: What It Is, What It's Not

Bulimia is characterized by alternating episodes of binge eating and purging. A binge may be anything from a bag of chips to a whole bag of groceries, but what all binges have in common is that the sufferer feels out of control and unable to stop eating. The binge stops only when the person is physically unable to eat any more or when her feelings of guilt and self-loathing become so strong that the desire to purge takes over.

Purging most often takes the form of vomiting; the bulimic makes herself throw up in a desperate attempt to get rid of the food consumed during the binge. While some people stick their fingers down their throats to make themselves vomit, others use dangerous drugs intended only to induce vomiting after the accidental ingestion of poison. Some people also abuse laxatives or overexercise to keep themselves from gaining weight after a binge. In addition to bingeing and purging, some bulimics periodically deny themselves food for a day or more; this fasting is characteristic of another eating disorder, anorexia nervosa.

Bulimia and anorexia have long been considered "eating disorders." New thinking in this area, however, has led to the concept of "disordered eating," which is much more comprehensive. The difference in wording is subtle but important. "In the past, an 'eating disorder' was defined as either anorexia nervosa or bulimia nervosa," Dr. Aurelia Nattiv and Linda Lynch reported in the journal *The Physician and Sportsmedicine*. "The new concept of 'disordered eating' emphasizes the spectrum of abnormal eating behavior, with poor nutritional habits on one end, and anorexia and bulimia on the other." This broadening of the scope of potential problem areas has allowed doctors, coaches, and counselors to see other, seemingly less dangerous conditions that could lead to the extremes of anorexia or bulimia, and also to recognize that poor eating habits need not be as critical as persistent bulimia or anorexia to be serious and worthy of attention. In her book *Lost for Words: The Psychoanalysis of Anorexia and Bulimia,* Em Farrell estimates that an incredible 80 percent of all people are believed to be affected by borderline disordered eating, known technically as subclinical eating disorder. That means that only 20 percent of all people—just one in five—have a healthy attitude toward food.

Bulimia and anorexia are technically mental disorders, but their consequences are physical. The mental illnesses known as "eating disorders" are responsible for more deaths than any other psychiatric condition. The National Institute of Mental

Health (NIMH) reports that one in ten anorexics die from the condition, either from the starvation, from complications such as heart attacks, or from suicide. The overall mortality rate for eating disorder sufferers who do not receive treatment is estimated at 10 to 20 percent. Sufferers are usually adolescent girls and young women between the ages of twelve and twenty-five, although both diseases are becoming more common in younger girls and may begin or persist well into adulthood. A growing body of research indicates that the number of male victims is also increasing, but current estimates state that between 90 and 95 percent of eating disorder sufferers are female.

Formal diagnosis of bulimia and anorexia is made based on a set of criteria in the *Diagnostic and Statistical Manual of Mental Disorders* (DSM), a guidebook used by mental health professionals. In order to be considered anorexic according to the DSM, a person must be at least 15 percent lighter than the minimum body weight for her height; to be diagnosed a bulimic, she must average at least two binge-and-purge sessions per week for at least three months. In addition to these factors, other conditions must also be met in regard to the victim's self-image and attitude toward food.

In her book *Lost for Words: The Psychoanalysis of Anorexia and Bulimia,* Em Farrell estimates that an incredible 80 percent of all people are believed to be affected by borderline disordered eating, known technically as subclinical eating disorder. That means that only 20 percent of all people—just one in five—have a healthy attitude toward food.

BINGE-EATING DISORDER

Anorexia and bulimia have long been considered the two most serious forms of disordered eating. However, a third eating disorder has recently been recognized. Called binge-eating disorder, or BED, it is similar to bulimia in that the person is unable to keep from consuming large amounts of food at one time, but unlike bulimia, the person does not purge the food. Therefore, most people suffering from BED, also known as compulsive eating, are overweight or obese. An estimated 30 percent of people participating in medically supervised weight control programs are found to be suffering from BED, compared to an average of 2 percent of the population overall. Like anorexia and bulimia, BED is most common among females; but more males are affected by it than by any other eating disorder. BED sufferers feel overwhelming shame at being unable to control their eating, and are also likely to have low self-esteem or suffer from depression. It is important to recognize that the inability to keep from overeating is not just gluttony or laziness—it is a disease, and its sufferers, like those of any other disease, need help to overcome it.

According to these guidelines, an estimated 2 to 3 percent of girls and young women are bulimic and another 1 percent are anorexic. It is important to point out, however, that many more people are currently struggling with disordered eating and suffering the physical, mental, and emotional consequences of these diseases, even if they do not yet fit the textbook definition of a person who suffers from anorexia or bulimia.

HOW IT STARTS

When you look in a mirror, what do you see? When you catch a glimpse of yourself in a store window, how do you react? A person with a healthy self-image will sometimes think she looks good, other times that she looks tired or even ill, and sometimes might even think, "How could I have left the house with my hair looking like THAT?!?" Overall, though, a person with a positive image of her physical self recognizes that she has days when she looks her best and days when she doesn't, and that either way it's not a reflection of her worth as a person. What the bulimic sees in the mirror is very different.

I went to the mall yesterday with my best friend who is way thinner than me, and she talked me into trying on bathing suits. I was so embarrassed! My butt is so huge, and my thighs are so puffy, and she's such a twig. I mean, she's a size four and I am double her size! She said I looked good, but I know she was just trying to be nice. There is NO WAY I'm going swimming this summer, at least not until I lose about fifty pounds!"

A person with a negative body image bases her worth on her appearance, and her appearance is never good enough for her. If she is overweight, or even if she truly is not overweight but thinks she is, she believes that if she could just lose the extra weight she would be popular and happy. If she gets a bad grade she might tell herself that she's just a loser, obviously—"How could I expect to do well in school when I can't even control my body?" Everything from acne to fights with parents is seen as a result of her weight. When you have a negative body image, it seems that all of your problems eventually lead back to your appearance. When that obsession with looking good is focused mainly on being "thin enough," an eating disorder is often the result.

But where does a negative body image come from? People aren't born hating the way they look. What influences a girl's self-image so strongly that she will resort to harming her body in a misguided effort to make it match her ideal?

WHAT SOCIETY SAYS

A girl born today has a lot to learn about what society expects of her. By the time she enters kindergarten, she is aware of what "pretty" means, and as she begins to interact with other children she quickly discovers where she stands in the pecking order of attractiveness. Her parents may already have told her that she is "a little doll," "cute as a button," with

HOW CAN I CHECK MY SELF-ESTEEM AND BODY IMAGE?

Ask yourself:

⊙ Do I feel inadequate after reading a teen or women's magazine?

⊙ Do I think it's okay for people to be proud of their accomplishments?

⊙ If I had all the money in the world, would I spend it on plastic surgery to enhance my body?

⊙ Do I think anyone can be thin if they just try hard enough?

⊙ Do I think I'm better than kids who are less attractive than me? Do I think more attractive people are better than me?

⊙ Do I feel unworthy of the attention of older or more popular kids?

⊙ Is there something that's unique about me that I am proud of or glad to have?

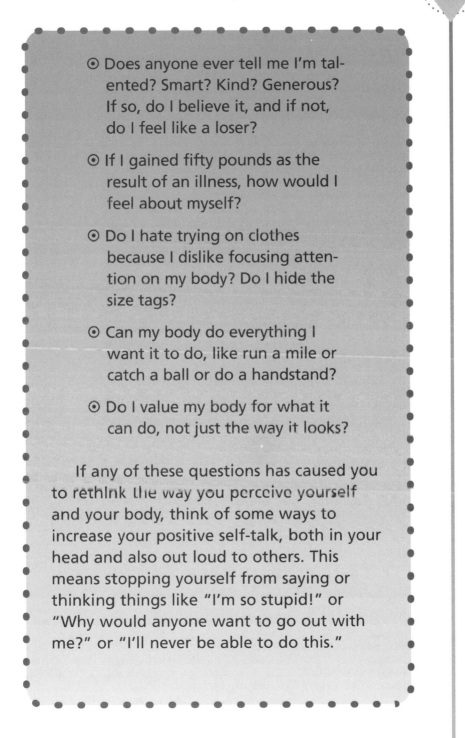

- ⊙ Does anyone ever tell me I'm talented? Smart? Kind? Generous? If so, do I believe it, and if not, do I feel like a loser?

- ⊙ If I gained fifty pounds as the result of an illness, how would I feel about myself?

- ⊙ Do I hate trying on clothes because I dislike focusing attention on my body? Do I hide the size tags?

- ⊙ Can my body do everything I want it to do, like run a mile or catch a ball or do a handstand?

- ⊙ Do I value my body for what it can do, not just the way it looks?

If any of these questions has caused you to rethink the way you perceive yourself and your body, think of some ways to increase your positive self-talk, both in your head and also out loud to others. This means stopping yourself from saying or thinking things like "I'm so stupid!" or "Why would anyone want to go out with me?" or "I'll never be able to do this."

"lovely hair" and "big beautiful eyes"—those are the things people tend to say in praise of little girls; in contrast, when people compliment little boys, they usually remark on how strong or smart they are. Naturally, children love attention and want to please their parents, so they try to live up to these compliments. In children's simple way of seeing things, little girls may equate their parents' love with their own beauty. So if another child tells a young girl that she is ugly, she may be petrified that if this is true, her parents will soon stop loving her.

As she moves through the early grades in school, the young girl becomes even more aware of how her appearance affects other people. If she is a pretty girl, she may find that the boys pay more attention to her and that the teachers are nicer to her. If she is average or unattractive, the girl will notice that prettier girls get more attention and seem to have it easier in life. Many studies have shown that attractive people are more easily accepted in our society and are believed to be smarter and more successful than their less attractive peers. In most cases these judgments are made subconsciously: The person forms his or her opinion based on the other person's looks but does not realize it. This is the origin of the saying "Don't judge a book by its cover."

By fourth or fifth grade, the girl's personality will have been influenced by her opinion of herself and her perception of how

A GIRL'S WORST FEAR

According to an article by Judith Newman in *Redbook*, young girls today are more afraid of becoming fat than they are of nuclear war, cancer, or losing their parents.

others view her. She may be outgoing or shy depending on how her attempts to interact with others have been received. She will probably have developed some insecurities by now—something every adolescent goes through—but how she reacts to her changing body and to others' assessments of her will form the basis of her self-image and will have a dramatic impact on the rest of her life.

As she finishes elementary school and moves on to junior high or high school, the girl, now a teenager, will have given a lot of thought to her worth as a person. As she has matured, she may have begun to see that there are things besides looks, including loyalty, generosity, and kindness, that make a person good or bad. Where physical attractiveness fits into her personal list of important traits will have been influenced by her friends and classmates, parents and siblings, teachers and coaches, and by a massive group of people that she has never met: the media.

THE MEDIA MACHINE

The "media" refers to all of the print, radio, and television news organizations in our country, and by extension the entertainment industry. It is very unfortunate that journalism and entertainment have merged to such an unhealthy extent, because journalism, in its purest form, is supposed to be an unbiased, neutral presentation of the facts of a story. As news organizations began to recognize the value of advertising to finance their operations, they became more and more dependent upon it, and soon the line between simply reporting the news

HOW SOCIETY SEES . . .
BILL CLINTON

Shortly after he began his first term as president of the United States, Bill Clinton became the butt of many media jokes for his love of McDonald's food and his efforts to keep himself in shape by jogging. Newspapers printed photo after unflattering photo of the president in running shorts and baggy T-shirts with captions suggesting that if he would just lay off the Big Macs he wouldn't have to run.

Why were the new president's eating and fitness habits of such interest to the media? Unlike a movie star, whose job is simply to entertain us, the president is entrusted with protecting the safety and welfare of the country. His performance in that capacity has little to do with the size of his waist. So why the focus on his appearance? Part of the answer to that question lies in the workings of the political world. Politicians know that their opinions on the "issues" are not the only thing that gets them elected; their ability to relate to the common person and to

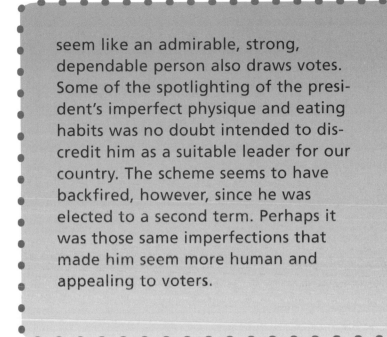

seem like an admirable, strong, dependable person also draws votes. Some of the spotlighting of the president's imperfect physique and eating habits was no doubt intended to discredit him as a suitable leader for our country. The scheme seems to have backfired, however, since he was elected to a second term. Perhaps it was those same imperfections that made him seem more human and appealing to voters.

versus reporting it in a way that made their advertisers look good began to blur. Now it's sometimes hard to tell whether you're watching a news program or a paid advertisement. Companies with something to sell often place full-page ads in newspapers and magazines made to look just like a news story or feature article. Few sporting events would happen without sponsors, companies that pay to have their logo prominently displayed in the arena or worn by the players. The most blatant example of this is auto racing, where drivers are coached to wear caps with their sponsor's logo and find a way to say the sponsor's name every time a camera and microphone are put in front of them. Such promotional tactics are also common in movies; when an actor takes a drink of Coke or Pepsi in a movie, it's not because the character prefers it—it's because Coke or Pepsi paid for the right to have its logo displayed in that film.

All of this is not inherently bad, but it is incredibly manipulative. Many worthwhile causes would get little attention without corporate sponsorship or the sale of advertising space, but the help comes with strings attached: When you have a sponsor, you are expected to help your sponsor gain new customers.

The important thing to know as a consumer in American society—and you became a consumer the very first time you asked your parents to buy you something—is the motivation behind all the commercials, magazine and newspaper ads, and prominent displays of brand-name items that you see every day. Companies don't really know what is best for you, and they don't know how to make you popular, witty, or pretty; they can't make your life trouble-free. But they want you to think that that's what buying their products will do for you! Their goal is to make money. They make money when you buy something of theirs. Therefore, they want you to buy their stuff, whether you need it or not. Some companies don't care that their products could injure you or make you sick—they just want your money. This is what the recent controversy over cigarette advertising is all about. In most cases, however, advertisers justify their hard-sell methods with the assertion that buying and using something you don't need won't actually harm you. Other than the bite it takes out of your savings, you might think this is true. But is it?

THE BARBIE EFFECT

For several years now, a grassroots effort has been under way to reveal the negative effects of the Barbie doll on girls' self-esteem. Once considered a simple, harmless toy, the Barbie doll is now seen by many people as a dangerous influence on young girls. It may seem like "just a dumb doll," but Barbie has become much more than that. Have you ever noticed that when people talk about Barbie, they refer to her the way they would a real person? They say "she" instead of "it," and talk about buying "her" clothes and cars and a house. Does anyone say, "I'm going out to throw Baseball with my friends," or "I want a new basket for Bike"? No, of course not. Why? Because we don't assign human traits or characteristics to toys like baseballs and bikes, but we do to dolls. The word for it is "anthropomorphizing," defined as "attributing human shape or characteristics to a god, animal, or inanimate [nonliving] thing." It is this anthropomorphizing of the Barbie doll that has many people worried.

When a girl sees Barbie as a representation of an adult woman, she begins to think that that is what she should grow up to be. If she saw no similarities between herself and Barbie, there would be no problem. No one worries about a kid who wants to become an alien from *Star Wars* when he or she grows up, because we all know that's impossible and the child will eventually realize that fact. The problem with wanting to be just like Barbie when you grow up is that many people do believe it is an attainable goal. Barbie has blond hair: You can have blond hair (by using hair color). Barbie has blue eyes: You can have blue eyes (colored contact lenses). Barbie has a tiny waist, full breasts, high cheekbones, and a perfectly toned butt: You too can have all of these things (with thousands of dollars of plastic surgery). Furthermore, besides being seen as an *attainable* goal, wanting to be just like Barbie is seen as an *admirable* goal. Even if parents say otherwise, the huge media machine continues to show us actresses, singers, and models who look just like Barbie! Our society may *say* that it's great to be yourself and people will love you just the way you are, but its actions say the opposite in a much more powerful way. When a girl finds that she does not measure up to society's ideal, her self-esteem plunges and the door is opened for all sorts of problems, from low grades and unhealthy friendships to severely self-destructive behaviors such as drug and alcohol use, and even psychological illnesses such as eating disorders.

HOW FAMILIES CAN HELP—AND HURT

By the time a typical girl reaches her teen years, she will have been bombarded with powerful messages about her self-worth, either directly, through the opinions of her friends and family and through her grades in school, or indirectly, through what she sees in the media and through what her friends, family, and classmates *don't* tell her. If a child does not receive consistent positive reinforcement, it is unlikely that she will develop a positive self-image. If her parents do not regularly tell her that she is a good and worthwhile person, she may very well assume that she is not. Since there are no tests for people to pass before they have children and no training is required, parents have no easy way of knowing whether they are doing a good job. While most parents mean well and want the best for their children, many simply don't know what they need to do in order to raise a child with a healthy self-image. And too often, parents are distracted or overwhelmed by issues of their own—financial worries, health problems, trouble at work, perhaps even marital difficulties. A bad situation at home, such as a seriously ill family member or financial trouble that threatens the loss of the house, does have a profound impact on the children, even if parents attempt to shield them from it. And sometimes the parents themselves are the problem—many children have the misfortune of watching their parents constantly fight or get a divorce, or of being born to alcoholics, drug users, or parents who are physically, emotionally, or sexually abusive. Each of these situations causes extreme stress in the child, whether that child realizes it or not, and any of those stressors could spark disordered eating.

THE LAST STRAW: WHAT TRIGGERS BULIMIA

Simply put, it could be anything. Often the trigger is a milestone or life change, such as the onset of puberty, starting high school or college, or getting married; it may also be a divorce or remarriage of the bulimic's parents, a serious illness, the death of a loved one, or some other traumatic family event. The beginning of bulimic behavior can be compared to a tornado: In order for it to start, a number of conditions must come together in the right combination and at the right time, but once those conditions are there, some sort of storm is inevitable.

The first time I made myself throw up was at a dance. I had eaten a piece of cake, and then I felt stupid sitting there with no one to dance with, so I went and got another piece. After that, I still felt stupid sitting there plus I felt disgusted with myself for pigging out. I went in the bathroom, and I heard someone throwing up. But before I could leave, she came out. When she saw me standing there she said how much better she felt now that she wouldn't gain any weight from the cake. I asked her what she meant, and she told me what to do. Then we both went back to the dance. I was happy because I had made a new friend and I didn't have to be there alone.

I started purging by accident. One time I was at a sleepover, and we all ate way too much junk food, and I got so sick that I threw up. It didn't feel good to do it, but it felt so much better after! Then one day a few weeks later, I was feeling guilty for eating a bag of chips after school, and I just decided to see if I could make myself get rid of it. It worked, and so now every time I eat something I shouldn't, I puke it back up.

My stepfather has always made fun of me and my sister for being fat. I hate eating dinner because he insists that we all sit together and

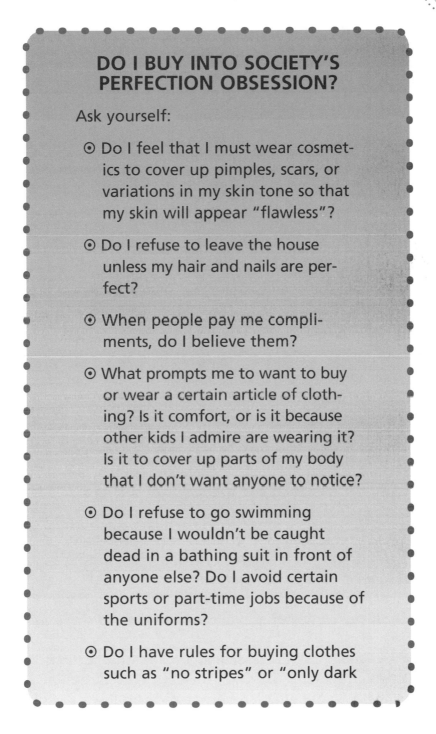

DO I BUY INTO SOCIETY'S PERFECTION OBSESSION?

Ask yourself:

⊙ Do I feel that I must wear cosmetics to cover up pimples, scars, or variations in my skin tone so that my skin will appear "flawless"?

⊙ Do I refuse to leave the house unless my hair and nails are perfect?

⊙ When people pay me compliments, do I believe them?

⊙ What prompts me to want to buy or wear a certain article of clothing? Is it comfort, or is it because other kids I admire are wearing it? Is it to cover up parts of my body that I don't want anyone to notice?

⊙ Do I refuse to go swimming because I wouldn't be caught dead in a bathing suit in front of anyone else? Do I avoid certain sports or part-time jobs because of the uniforms?

⊙ Do I have rules for buying clothes such as "no stripes" or "only dark colors" that I believe enhance my figure?

⊙ Would I exercise as much as I do now if appearance did not matter in our society?

⊙ Do I suck in my stomach when someone I consider attractive walks by?

⊙ Do I feel uncomfortable eating in front of others, even if I feel hungry? Does it depend on whether the food is "good" or "bad"?

watches every bite we eat. Mom loads our plates up and then says we have to eat it all, but he makes faces at us, like puffing his cheeks out and making pig noises, so we just hurry up and eat to get away from him. My sister taught me a trick, though—we just wolf down our food and then watch TV for a few minutes till Mom is doing the dishes, and then we go to the bathroom and help each other throw up. That way we don't get yelled at for not eating but we don't have to worry about gaining weight.

In each of these cases, the bulimic behavior began when the girl's self-esteem was threatened by the idea of being fat, something about which she was already hypersensitive. There may have been some other contributing factor that led to her first purge as well—a bad grade, a teacher's critical remark, a snub from a friend or a boy in school, a parent's angry look over some small thing. The point is that when a girl has a negative body image and by extension low self-esteem, sooner or later something is likely to send her into disordered eating and possibly into bulimia, anorexia, or binge-eating disorder.

THE REALITIES OF PURGING

While the bulimic's goal is to be thin and attractive, the methods she uses are far from pretty. The most common way a bulimic purges is by forcing herself to vomit.

I'm forty-five minutes into my latest binge and that feeling is starting again. I know in a few minutes I will puke this all back up. I go into the bathroom to get ready. I put my hair in a clip so it won't get dirty, and I lift the toilet seat and wipe the rim with window cleaner so maybe I won't get too many germs on my face. I pace a little bit, back and forth in front of the toilet, feeling the pressure build in my stomach and wishing I could do this some other way, but it's too late now, I ate it and it's got to come up. I kneel down and feel the cold of the toilet bowl against my knees, brace myself with one hand and jam the other into my mouth, as far back in my throat as I can. My body jerks and I nick my knuckle on my teeth again, and this time I don't get my hand out of the way fast enough, so I hold it dripping over the bowl while I get reacquainted with the Doritos, the chocolate cookies, the candy, the cheese and crackers. Sometimes I close my eyes, but sometimes I don't, and this time seeing the orange and brown slop with whole M&Ms in it makes me heave even more. I remember for about the fiftieth time that I ought to wear my headphones so I won't have to hear myself. When nothing much is coming up any more, I grab the sink and stand up, rinse off my crusty hand, and hop on the scale. No change. I hate myself for bingeing, but I always make sure I take care of it right away, and every time it feels like walking out of confession with a clean slate.

Over time, repeated vomiting causes tooth enamel to erode, allowing decay to set in and requiring extensive dental work. The teeth tend to become discolored, particularly the front teeth. Bulimia causes painful, chronic digestive problems—diarrhea and/or constipation, even stomach ulcers. It causes the glands around the face to become enlarged, making the cheeks puffy. When the fingers are used to provoke the vomiting, cuts and scarring on the fingers and hands are common. Vomiting causes dehydration and life-threatening imbalances in the body's electrolytes. It can result in menstrual irregularities, kidney damage, irregular heartbeat, and seizures. It can cause death from the damage inflicted on the heart and other organs, from the many chemical imbalances it causes in the body, and in some cases even from a ruptured stomach or esophagus.

Bulimics also frequently abuse laxatives in an attempt to force the food to rush through their systems without being absorbed. This often leaves them constantly constipated or suffering from such severe diarrhea that they are unable to control their bowel movements at all. Diet pills and diuretics that rid the body of water are also popular ways to quickly drop a few pounds, but they too cause havoc in the body's complex chemical systems.

Compulsive exercise is another method employed by both bulimics and anorexics. Overexercising often goes unnoticed by the bulimic's family and friends, especially if she is involved in sports. In our society, a person who exercises regularly is considered praiseworthy; few people recognize that it is possible, and unhealthy, to work out too much. For more on this element of bulimia, see the section Most at Risk: Young Women and the Female Athlete Triad in Chapter 2.

WHY IT DOESN'T WORK

Bulimia is actually a coping mechanism, the mind's attempt to call attention to a problem or problems through the physical manifestations of illness and extreme behavior. A person who lacks the ability to speak up for her needs or to assert her value as a unique human being may develop an eating disorder as a means of expressing feelings of self-doubt, shame, grief, or anger; she may binge to bury her painful feelings, but then immediately purge when she finds herself overwhelmed by negative emotions associated with the possibility of gaining weight. The bulimic's "cry for help" is not a conscious decision on her part; she does not binge and purge simply to gain attention or pity. In fact, she may not even know why she does it. Bulimic behavior is a subconscious warning to the sufferer to notice and tend to her psychological pain. It is this complex blend of emotional issues that makes bulimia and other eating disorders difficult to treat; in order to recover, the bulimic must address and learn to manage these issues, and ultimately learn to accept and love herself as she is, while also learning to meet the physical needs of her body.

So, as a coping mechanism, bulimia doesn't work, but it also doesn't work on another level. Ironically, the bulimic's goal of being physically perfect and model-thin is not well served by purging. Most bulimics believe that when they purge the excess calories consumed in a binge, they have prevented themselves from gaining any weight as a consequence of the binge and may even lose weight. But after a while, the body is not so easily outsmarted. Dietitian Joanne Larsen points out in her Web site, "Ask the Dietitian," that "frequent and regular vomiting does not cause weight loss. Your body learns to adjust and starts digesting food higher in the digestive tract because it learns that it can't hold onto the food very long. Also, food stays in the bulimic's stomach much longer because of the frequent vomiting. Bulimic patients have told me of vomiting food they ate almost twenty-four hours before."

HOW IT ENDS

Bulimia is not something that will just go away with time.

> *Margaret is an investment broker, a wife, and the mother of three children, only two of whom are still alive. Her daughter Ashley died after three years as a bulimic. "I knew she did it," Margaret says. "I did it too when I was her age. I just figured she would outgrow it like I did." But Margaret didn't really outgrow bulimia; she only changed her tactics. When she could no longer stand the pain in her throat that self-induced vomiting caused, Margaret vowed to stop purging. She resisted for three weeks, but then her grandmother died and Margaret began bingeing again. Still, she managed to keep from purging and gradually gained ten pounds. That was when she discovered diet pills and laxatives. Ashley learned her obsession with her weight, and the many tricks she used to control it, from her mother.*

Left untreated, bulimia causes progressively more serious health problems that can eventually be fatal. There is no "safe" way to be bulimic. Therefore, while bulimia can go on for years, it can only

Left untreated, bulimia causes progressively more serious health problems that can eventually be fatal. There is no "safe" way to be bulimic.

end in one of two ways: treatment, through a combination of self-education and professional help, or death.

BULIMIA VS. ANOREXIA

Yeah, I know a girl who's anorexic. She was looking really good for a while, but now she's way too skinny—looks like some refugee or something. There's another girl that one of the other guys says does that bulimia thing, but she's fat, so I figure a bulimic is just an anorexic who doesn't try hard enough.

That comparison, while cruel and extremely insensitive, is the common way to think of the similarities and differences between the disorders.

The warning signs of anorexia include losing a significant amount of weight and continuing to diet after becoming thin; feeling fat even after losing weight; having a strong fear of gaining weight; losing one's monthly periods; being preoccupied with food, calorie-counting, nutritional content, or cooking; exercising compulsively; and even bingeing and purging.

The most obvious difference between bulimia and anorexia is the victim's weight. While a bulimic is usually at or near her normal weight, an anorexic is by definition at least 15 percent below her healthy weight. Anorexics also develop physical problems that are different from those that plague bulimics. For example, a thin layer of hair, called lanugo hair, will grow over the anorexic's entire body as a reaction to her self-induced starvation. The American

Anorexia/Bulimia Association estimates that 1,000 anorexics die each year from their illness.

It is possible to have both anorexia and bulimia at the same time, and it is common to alternate between the two. It is believed that up to 50 percent of bulimics are former anorexics. Those eating disorder sufferers who show symptoms of both anorexia and bulimia are at the greatest risk of permanent health complications or death.

BULIMIA VS. BINGE-EATING DISORDER (BED)

Bulimic? Dang, I wish I could be bulimic! All I ever do is eat, and I can't stop myself. It's like, sometimes I'll think about a candy bar and tell myself, "You don't need that," but then I just seem to, I don't know, just forget all the reasons not to eat It. So I eat it and then maybe after I'm done I might start to remember why I shouldn't have eaten it, but while I'm doing it I have no willpower. And the thought of making myself throw it back up just doesn't appeal to me. I don't even have enough willpower to do that.

It is very likely that a person who suffers from binge-eating disorder, also known as compulsive eating, doesn't know that his or her problem has a name other than "laziness" or "gluttony" or "weakness." Traditionally in our society, overweight people, perceived as unable or unwilling to control their eating, have been ridiculed, laughed at, scorned, and shunned. They get lectures from doctors, suspicion from employers, and disgust from love interests, but they provide themselves with the worst feedback: self-loathing, guilt, and shame. Being overweight because of medical problems, lack of exercise, or ignorance of proper nutrition is hard enough to live with, but believing that it is your own fault is even worse. And most binge eaters are overweight; in fact, it is estimated that 30 to 40 percent of obese people suffer from BED.

Some of the symptoms of binge-eating disorder include being overweight; having episodes of eating that you feel unable to stop; eating when you're not actually hungry; being secretive about what you eat and how much, or waiting until you are alone to eat; frequent dieting and weight fluctuations; awareness that your eating habits are not normal; feeling depressed frequently; and having successes or failures at work or in your personal life that you attribute to your weight. The most obvious difference between BED and bulimia is that the binge eater does not vomit, use laxatives, overexercise, or use any other method to purge the excess calories after a binge.

Approximately 2 percent of the population is believed to be suffering from BED. Binge-eating disorder occurs much more frequently in males than do the other eating disorders; it is estimated that 40 percent of BED sufferers are male.

Who Has Bulimia?

The typical bulimic is an average-weight or slightly overweight female between the ages of fifteen and thirty-five. The American Anorexia/Bulimia Association (AABA) reports that 5 percent of adolescent and adult women have anorexia, bulimia, or binge-eating disorder. It is hypothesized that the vast majority of eating disorder sufferers are female because society places a much greater burden of physical perfection on women than it does on men. It is estimated that one of every 250 girls between the ages of twelve and eighteen has struggled with an eating disorder at some time, but it is impossible to know for sure because not everyone asks for or receives help, and doctors are not required to report the number of eating disorder cases they treat.

DOES BULIMIA AFFECT ONLY WHITE AMERICANS?

Eating disorders were long believed to affect only white girls and young women, and some researchers speculate that, in the past, cultural differences did indeed protect black, Hispanic, Asian, and Native American females from bulimia and anorexia. Now, however, greater numbers of nonwhite females are coming forward to find help for disordered eating. No conclusions have yet been reached on whether this trend indicates an actual rise in eating disorders among nonwhite women or simply an increase in the reporting of them. What is certain, however, is that nonwhite women are no longer being ignored as at risk for eating disorders. Conscientious scientists and doctors recognize that all girls and young women, regardless of race, are in danger of developing disordered eating habits as a result of the same societal pressures that afflict white females.

While the United States reports one of the highest rates of disordered eating in the world, other countries are not immune to the problem. Japan and China have seen a rise in anorexia and bulimia, but the shame associated with psychotherapy in those countries prevents many women from seeking treatment, so accurate measurement or even estimation of the extent of the problem there is impossible. Argentina's incidences of both conditions are three times as high as in the United States; the crisis of disordered eating in that country is attributed to a societal obsession with physical perfection that is even worse than ours.

WHAT ABOUT MALES?

Males are estimated to make up only 5 to 10 percent of all eating disorder sufferers. Approximately one million males, or 1 percent of the population, have bulimia, anorexia, or binge-eating disorder, according to the AABA. The number of reported cases is growing, however, as men learn that eating disorders are not just "women's diseases." Many men, especially heterosexuals, are still reluctant to seek help for anorexia or bulimia because in recent years the number of homosexual men seeking help for disordered eating has increased; it seems that many straight men are embarrassed to admit to the problem and are afraid that if they seek help they will be labeled gay. In reality, there is no known correlation between sexual preference and risk of disordered eating; being gay doesn't cause bulimia, and having bulimia can't make anyone "turn gay." The higher reporting rate among gay men probably indicates that they are more willing to request help, not that more gays than straights are eating disorder sufferers.

Some preliminary research indicates that males may be more at risk than females for binge-eating disorder. In our culture, men are expected to have a "healthy appetite," so when a male eats an entire pizza by himself in one sitting, few people see it as a warning sign. If a female were to do that, however, it would be much more likely to raise a red flag. While the female would probably be embarrassed and ashamed, the male would be inclined to brag about his feat.

WHAT ABOUT ABUSED KIDS?

Being stuck in an abusive or neglectful situation can certainly trigger disordered eating. However, research so far has not found a cause-and-effect

DOES COMPETITIVE WRESTLING ENCOURAGE BULIMIA?

In the last few years, the weight-cutting practices used by high school and college wrestlers have received a lot of attention and have prompted concern over their effects on the health of the young men using them. Some coaches and wrestlers believe that shedding as many pounds as possible right before a meet in order to compete in a lower weight class is a good way to gain an advantage over opponents. The strategy is dangerous, however, and sometimes fatal: The use of diuretics, rubber suits, steam rooms, and overexercising have been listed as the cause of death for several wrestlers in recent years, and these practices are believed to lead to disordered eating in many more young men. Cornell wrestling coach Rob Koll says a much better strategy is to build muscle mass through strength training: "We'd like to have a guy get stronger and become a good wrestler rather than a good weight cutter."

relationship between child abuse and eating disorders in the victim. This means that children who suffer physical, emotional, or sexual abuse may be more vulnerable to disordered eating, in the same way any child in a dangerous, unstable, or explosive environment is vulnerable. Researchers have not demonstrated, however, that abused children are in any more danger of becoming bulimic or anorexic than anyone else solely because of the abuse.

MOST AT RISK: YOUNG WOMEN AND THE FEMALE ATHLETE TRIAD

There is growing concern among those who work with female athletes over a set of three conditions now known as the Female Athlete Triad. Consisting of amenorrhea (the loss of one's monthly period), disordered eating, and osteoporosis (loss of density and increased brittleness of the bones), the condition is extremely dangerous and potentially fatal—and alarmingly common. While an estimated 1 percent of the female population is considered anorexic and another 2 to 3 percent are bulimic, various studies have found that anywhere from 15 to 70 percent of female athletes practice pathogenic, or disease-causing, weight-control behaviors that in some cases include anorexia and/or bulimia. Nattiv and Lynch emphasized in their essay for *The Physician and Sportsmedicine,* "Although they may not fit the . . . criteria for anorexia or bulimia, they are still at risk for developing serious psychiatric, endocrine, and skeletal problems."

Approximately 2 to 5 percent of women in the

general population have amenorrhea, but its prevalence among female athletes is estimated at anywhere from 3.4 percent to 66 percent, depending on the study's definition of the condition and the characteristics of its subject group. While there are many possible causes for amenorrhea (including the most obvious—pregnancy), in a female athlete the condition should alert the young woman's doctor or coach to evaluate her closely for disordered eating and osteoporosis. Even if the other elements of the triad can be ruled out, amenorrhea should not be considered "normal" and allowed to continue without a thorough search for its cause. While it once was believed that simply dipping below a certain percentage of body fat could cause a young woman's periods to stop even though she was otherwise fit and healthy, and was therefore not serious, further research has begun to show that the situation is not that simple. It is important to understand that amenorrhea is not healthy, even though the young woman experiencing it may welcome the convenience of not having a period each month and may even believe, falsely, that losing her period is a point of pride and indicates overall fitness.

Most people who hear the term "osteoporosis" think of very old women with hunched backs, weak joints, and bones that break with just one fall. Young women do not consider themselves at risk for the condition, and in fact it is not common for a normal woman to develop it in her younger years. However, the combination of disordered eating and amenorrhea puts a young woman, even a teenager or woman in her twenties, at serious risk for loss of bone density. This loss is presently believed to be

TIME OUT:
DOES YOUR COACH KNOW
WHAT'S GOOD FOR YOU?

If you are an athlete and your coach pressures you to lose weight in unhealthy ways, don't go along with him or her. Show your coach this book and point out that you believe it would be unhealthy for you to weigh any less than you do now. If your coach won't listen to you, don't just drop the subject. Switch to another sport, or, if you really love the one you're in, talk to another coach, your parents, or a counselor about ways you can continue to participate in your sport while resisting the coach's bad advice. Remember that your coach probably does not intend to hurt you, but is fixated on winning and needs to learn about the dire consequences of disordered eating and unhealthy weight loss. Speaking up for yourself will keep you safe and may prevent that coach from harming other athletes as well.

irreversible, meaning that the woman's skeleton, which may not have even finished growing, will never again be as strong as it was before the condition set in. She will be prone to stress fractures and other breaks that aren't even caused by an accident or fall. Far from being a strong athlete, she will be left permanently fragile and severely limited in the activities in which she can participate.

There is a sad irony involved in the problem of disordered eating and weight control among female athletes: Sometimes the tactics do improve performance. Loren Mooney reported in *Cornell Magazine* that in some sports, such as gymnastics and diving, a slimmer physique leads to higher scores for appearance, and in sports such as running and swimming, a lower body-fat percentage can improve endurance. "Some athletes trim down to a light, but natural, competition weight and improve their performance," Mooney noted. "Others can cross the fine line to become compulsive about weight loss." The key is finding an ideal weight for performance and health; this is something most adolescents are ill equipped to do on their own, and it's the reason a well-informed, attentive coach who demonstrates healthy priorities for his or her team is crucial to every athlete's success and well-being. The emphasis should always be on maintaining overall wellness; if there is even the slightest possibility that reducing body-fat percentage may be unhealthy for an athlete, it should be discouraged. The bottom line? Work hard to reach your goals, but never risk your health to be number one.

3 Helping Yourself, Helping Others

If you believe you are bulimic or suspect that a friend or family member may be, it is critically important to get help right away. Studies have shown that those who receive early treatment have a better chance for full recovery than those whose condition persists for years. Left untreated, bulimia can have irreversible consequences and can even be fatal.

CAN I FIX THIS MYSELF?

If you believe that you suffer from disordered eating or recognize the symptoms of bulimia in yourself, you've taken the most important step in helping yourself: You've identified the problem. Reading this book is giving you a lot of information on your condition, including the dangerous consequences you will face if you don't find a way to stop it, and it has also given you much food for thought as to the reasons that you might have developed this problem.

HOW CAN I TELL IF I HAVE BULIMIA?

Ask yourself:

⊙ Do I think about food a lot, even when I'm not hungry?

⊙ Do I prefer eating alone?

⊙ Do I count every calorie I consume, even in chewing gum? Do I meticulously inspect and examine my food for any signs that something is wrong with it?

⊙ Am I happy with myself?

⊙ Do I diet frequently?

⊙ Have I ever used laxatives or diuretics (water pills) in an attempt to lose weight?

⊙ Do I ever "lose control" and eat a much larger than normal amount of food at one time?

⊙ Do I have irregular periods, or none at all?

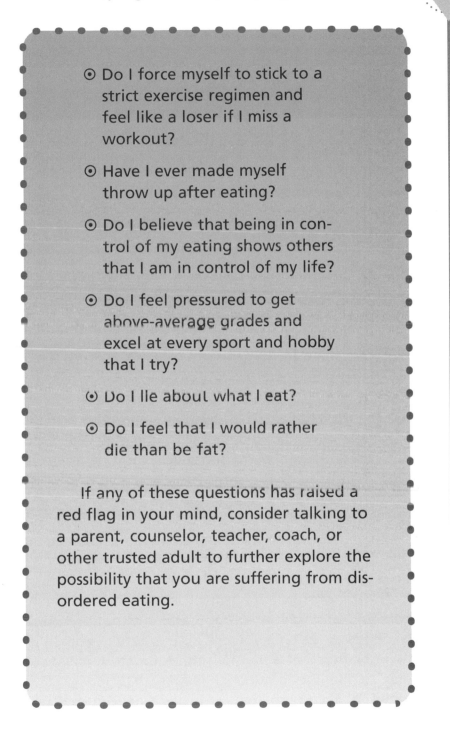

⊙ Do I force myself to stick to a strict exercise regimen and feel like a loser if I miss a workout?

⊙ Have I ever made myself throw up after eating?

⊙ Do I believe that being in control of my eating shows others that I am in control of my life?

⊙ Do I feel pressured to get above-average grades and excel at every sport and hobby that I try?

⊙ Do I lie about what I eat?

⊙ Do I feel that I would rather die than be fat?

If any of these questions has raised a red flag in your mind, consider talking to a parent, counselor, teacher, coach, or other trusted adult to further explore the possibility that you are suffering from disordered eating.

You can find many more books to read in the For Further Reading section at the end of this book; some of these sources might offer information more closely tailored to your individual situation.

If you believe that you are at risk for developing an eating disorder but don't have one yet, educating yourself may be all you need. Read everything you can find about disordered eating, and learn as much as you can about good nutrition and healthy exercise. Then make positive changes in your eating habits and your exercise routine. Remember that your self-esteem and body image are very important to your well-being; practice positive self-talk on a regular basis, and surround yourself with positive people who make you feel good about yourself. Speak out against unrealistic media images, and refuse to participate in "body bashing," even if all the popular kids are doing it. Always remember that you are a lovable, worthwhile person no matter what you look like, and anyone who values you only for your looks is not good for you. Celebrate your unique qualities, and encourage your friends to do the same for themselves. You can be a positive force in other people's lives as well.

Do you recall the distinction between disordered eating and eating disorders that was explained in the first chapter? While it is possible to correct disordered eating on your own, helping yourself recover from an eating disorder will be extremely difficult and perhaps impossible without professional help. Even if you are able to force yourself to stop bingeing and purging, no amount of willpower can erase the emotional issues that led you to bulimia. If you feel that you might need more help than you can find in books but you aren't ready to talk about it yet, it's okay to wait until you've thoroughly researched your problem and sorted out for yourself how you want to go about changing it before you tell your parents or ask another trusted adult for help, *as long as you are not in immediate danger.* If you are experiencing any disturbing physical symptoms, such as an irregular heartbeat, bleeding, fainting or dizzy spells, or pain, don't wait—tell someone and make it clear that you need immediate help. In any case, don't take too long to seek help. Make a commitment to yourself to ask for help two weeks from today, and use that time to finish this book and check out some more at the library, and to think through how you want to handle your recovery. If you wait longer than two weeks, though, you're procrastinating. Don't allow yourself to ignore this problem, and don't think it will just go away on its own—it won't! Give yourself a good, positive pep talk, then build up your courage and get a trusted adult involved.

Whether you choose to tell your parents first is up to you. You could start with a school counselor, a teacher, another relative, or by calling a hotline. The important thing is to start somewhere. Following are tips on talking to your parents as well as seeking professional help.

HOW TO TELL YOUR PARENTS

At some point during their teenage years, most people experience tension in their relationship with their parents. This is partly the result of the normal letting-go process that accompanies the transition to

HOW SOCIETY SEES . . .
OPRAH WINFREY

Oprah Winfrey, the host of one of the most popular talk shows on television today, has waged public war with her weight for years. Viewers have cheered her in her various dieting efforts, but some have been less supportive when she has regained the weight. Currently Oprah is at a healthy weight and fitness level, a feat she attributes to her commitment to exercise and healthy eating as outlined in her book *Make the Connection: Ten Steps to a Better Body and a Better Life*, coauthored with her trainer, Bob Greene. It is a testament to her strength as a person, however, that Oprah has managed to work past the constant scrutiny of the public and refocus their attention on her message of self-empowerment. "If you focus on what you have, you'll end up having more. If you focus on what you lack, you will never have enough. That is a guarantee," Oprah has remarked. "If you aim at nothing, you'll hit it every time."

adulthood: In some ways, teens are self-sufficient and capable of making their own decisions, but in other ways they are still very much in need of their parents' guidance. The difficulty comes in recognizing the difference between a situation you can handle yourself and one with which you need your parents to help you. Dealing with an eating disorder is an example of something you can't do alone, but unfortunately, many parents are ill-equipped to help their children in this area.

> *I have been bingeing and purging for three years now, and I finally told my parents a couple of weeks ago. They seemed to want to help me then, but now whenever I mention it they ignore me or get mad. One time my mother even said I was just doing this to get attention. I'm out of control and I know I need help, but I can't make myself stop on my own. I'm starting to wonder now if they really even care. How can I make them understand?*

If you have an eating disorder, you do need the love and support of your family to help you overcome it, but you also must take some responsibility in helping them to help you. Knowing how they might react to your news will help you to remain calm when you talk to them.

- ⊙ Anger. It is common and normal for parents to be angry at the situation, at themselves, and, unfortunately, even at their child when confronted with the news of an eating disorder. If this happens, remind yourself that they are probably most angry with themselves. They may say things like "Where did we go wrong?" or "Why are you doing this to us?," statements that could easily put you on the defensive, but try your best not to get angry yourself. Since most eating disorders develop at a time of upheaval and change in the life of the sufferer, it is very possible that yours was triggered by a family problem, but now is not the time to place blame. You don't have to give a reason for your problem—just tell them that it exists and that you need their help to overcome it. Give them time to "cool off," then choose a time when everyone is calm and relaxed to talk to them about how they can help you.

⊙ Sadness. Your parents will probably be very sad for you, for themselves, and for the family in general when you bring them your news. They may cry or apologize for not being better parents. They may even experience a temporary depression and express feelings of hopelessness, saying things like "Your life is ruined" or "How can we ever get through this?" If they do react this way, you will probably feel overwhelming guilt for causing them grief, but do not allow that guilt to stop you from asking for help. It would be natural for you to resolve to take care of your problem on your own in order to spare them the pain of seeing you suffer, but you must resist this impulse. No one's life is perfect, and no child is problem-free. Remember that your parents are there to help you when you need them, no matter how much it may hurt them. Reassure them that you will all get through this and things will be better—your life is not ruined—but for now, you must allow them to share your burden.

⊙ Fear. Another possibility is that your parents will become very frightened. They may even say things like "I can't handle this" or "This is too much for me." Single parents may find helping a child with an eating disorder even more challenging because they have no one to help them work through their own feelings. Consequently, they may turn to their children for the emotional support that a spouse would provide, further burdening the child at an already difficult time. If this is your situation, remember that you are the child, not the parent: you should not have to shoulder the responsibility of "fixing" this yourself. If your parent or parents seem unable to cope with your problem and are depending on you for emotional support, get another adult involved. A person who cares about you but is not as close to you as your parents is less likely to be paralyzed with fear and may be better able to help you.

⊙ Silence. Many people cannot find the words to express their feelings, so they simply say nothing. If your parents react this way, it does not mean that they don't care or that they don't love you. It could be that they just don't know what to say, or perhaps are afraid that they will say the wrong thing and hurt you. After you have found the courage to talk to them about your problem, this reaction will probably be very frustrating for you. If you feel you're not getting through face-to-face, try writing them a letter. This will allow you to clarify your thoughts and to say everything you want to say, and it will allow them time to absorb your words and to choose exactly what they want to say, or write, in response. In your letter, be sure to explain the ways in which your parents can help you, and ask them to give you a response within a certain amount of time (for example, within three days). Tell them that you know this is difficult for them, but it is a serious problem that won't just go away and you are counting on them to help you.

⊙ Embarrassment. Some people believe in keeping family members' problems within the family and not "airing their dirty laundry" by telling others. If your parents are this way, they might tell you not to discuss your eating disorder with anyone else. They may imply or even flat-out say that you should be ashamed of it and that if other people find out they will think less of you. This attitude is wrong—keeping problems and feelings to yourself is not healthy, and expressing them is nothing to be ashamed of—but if your parents feel this way you will have a hard time convincing them of that. As long as you know that an eating disorder is not shameful, you can cooperate with your parents so they will get you the help you need by not discussing your problem with neighbors, clergymembers at your local place of worship, or teachers or other school officials. If it enables you to see the doctors and therapists and other professionals you need to help you begin to recover, you may have to live with your parents' attitude. However, if they forbid you to discuss your problem with anyone *and* they fail to get help for you, then you will have to go against their wishes and take matters into your own hands. An eating disorder is an extremely serious threat to your health;

if your parents completely refuse to help you, you must find someone else who will, like a teacher, school counselor, coach, or even another relative. Keep in mind, however, that this may only be their first reaction; if you give them a few days to cool off and approach them again, you may find that they have changed their minds and want to help you.

If days or weeks go by after you've told your parents about your problem and they are still unable to get past their initial reaction, it's time to go to another adult. Telling a trusted guidance counselor, teacher, or doctor would be a good choice, and enlisting the help of another close relative may be an option as well. The important thing is that you find someone to help you. Your wellness is the top priority, and you must do whatever it takes to connect with the people who can help you begin to get better.

HOW TO GET PROFESSIONAL HELP

At various points in your healing process, you may need to enlist the help of a professional with experience in assisting sufferers from disordered eating. Now, you may think that no one can possibly know what this is like for you, and you are right: No one can know exactly what it feels like to be you. But that does not mean that no one can help you. There are many people who want to help people like you, and they have educated

DRUGS AND EATING DISORDER TREATMENT

Some mental health professionals use antidepressants as a tool in treating disordered eating. Since a person suffering from an eating disorder also often shows signs of depression, it is theorized that treating the depression with drugs such as Prozac, Zoloft, Paxil, or Elavil may also help to alleviate the eating disorder. The drug alone will not bring about a cure, however; therapy is still needed to work through the emotional problems that led to the eating disorder, but the drug may allow the patient to get more out of the therapy process. Not all therapists can prescribe medication: psychiatrists can, but psychologists cannot. When seeking treatment, be prepared to decide whether you would be comfortable including the use of an antidepressant in your recovery. If you decide to try it, ask questions about its possible side effects and learn as much as you can about what the drug is expected to do for you.

WHAT IF I'M NOT RICH?

It is true that professional help can be expensive. If you have no insurance, or if your insurance won't cover it and paying for such services is a problem for your family, there are low-cost and free programs to help you. They may be harder to find or may take longer to get into, but don't give up. Remember that overcoming your eating disorder is crucial to your health, so keep trying until you get help.

WHAT WILL "TREATMENT" BE LIKE?

There are a number of different approaches to treating bulimia. The best one for you should be based on the severity of your condition as well as your individual personality and the circumstances that brought about the problem in the first place. Since bulimia is a psychological illness but causes physical problems, you will most likely want to involve professionals from both the medical and mental health fields in your care.

If you are extremely ill, the first step might be spending some time in a hospital to stabilize your physical condition. If so, you can work out a step-by-step plan for your recovery while you're there, and you will probably meet many different people who can help you both in planning what to do and in carrying it out. Steps in your physical recovery may include visiting your primary care physician or family doctor to assess the damage to your body and decide how to repair it. Similarly, a trip to the dentist is a good idea to have a thorough exam and reverse any decay that may have begun as a result of purging. Another element in your physical healing is educating yourself in healthy eating habits. You may be referred to a dietitian or nutritionist for help in learning how to eat well and exercise in moderation to maintain a healthy body.

Your most difficult task will probably be your mental and emotional healing. This side of your recovery will most likely involve some sort of therapy, which may be one-on-one or together with your family members or other recovering bulimics. You may find that a combined approach—some individual sessions with a psychiatrist or psychologist combined with some family counseling and perhaps some group therapy or participation in a self-help group—will give you a good variety of useful insights. Whichever approach will be the most comfortable and effective for you is the best one to use.

There is no predictable time frame for recovery from bulimia. If you are in the beginning stages of the disease, you may be able to turn it around in a matter of weeks, but don't be discouraged if you find that your course of treatment is expected to take many months. Bulimia does not appear overnight; it grows slowly over time, and when you do finally realize that you have a problem, many facets of your life have already been changed and influenced by it. Therefore, bulimia cannot be cured overnight; it will take time for you to break old habits and train yourself to think and act in new, self-affirming ways.

REMEMBER, THEY'RE HUMAN, TOO

When you seek the services of a professional, whether it's a doctor, therapist, nutrition counselor, or trainer, remember that that person is a fallible human being just like yourself. Experts can make mistakes, and they can exercise poor judgment. It's okay for you to disagree with them or to question their reasons or sources of information. It is important for you to take an active role in healing yourself, and if someone advises you to do something that you think is wrong or that makes you uncomfortable, speak up. Discuss your discomfort. If the adviser becomes defensive and demands that you follow his or her orders, consider finding someone else to help you. (It may help to discuss the situation with your parents.) There are extreme cases in which a person must be hospitalized and treated against her will in order to keep her alive, but such situations are rare. In most cases, you will be allowed to have a voice in choosing the course of your treatment, and if you are truly committed to healing, the adults who are helping you should allow you to direct your recovery. If you feel that you are not being heard, speak up, and if you still are not taken seriously, find someone else to help you.

A FRIEND IN NEED: HELPING OTHERS TO PREVENT OR DEAL WITH AN EATING DISORDER

I have never forgotten the time in elementary school when a classmate of mine told our group of girls what her mother had said to her at dinner the night before. I forget how the subject came up, but I remember that she seemed stunned and very sad as she told us about it. It seems that her mother had made chicken and dumplings for dinner, and our friend asked for more. Her mother told her harshly that she was already too fat and didn't need another dumpling. I remember looking at her and thinking, My God, if she is fat, what am I? It's been over twenty years since this happened, but I have always wished that I had known what to say to that girl, and I have always wondered what became of her.

Often it is hard to know what to say when something like the above scenario happens. Many people are afraid of saying the wrong thing, but they can't imagine what the right thing to say would be, so they simply say nothing. Think back to a time when you told someone about something hurtful that happened to you and the other person didn't say anything. Did you feel heard? Did you feel that the other person cared about you? Most likely you felt ignored or rejected. The other person may have felt terrible for you, but that sympathy didn't do you any good because he or she couldn't express it. If you suspect a friend or family member is suffering from bulimia, find the courage to talk to her about it. It is

SOME QUESTIONS TO ASK WHEN CHOOSING A THERAPIST

The American Anorexia/Bulimia Association suggests asking the following questions when choosing a therapist to help you toward recovery from an eating disorder:

About the Therapist:

⊙ How did you get involved in treating eating disorders?

⊙ What percentage of your clients have eating disorders?

⊙ How much time will we spend focusing on food, weight, and diet issues?

⊙ Will you allow me to come to an appointment even if I have a relapse (binge/purge, overexercise, etc.)?

⊙ Do you believe people with eating disorders can be cured, or will I always have this disease?

⊙ What things should I know about you? Why should I see you?

About the Therapy Process:

- How would you describe your approach to therapy?

- What goals will we set?

- Will you involve my family in my recovery?

- Will you monitor my weight and what I eat?

- What can I expect during a session? How long will each session be, and how often will we meet?

- What do I have to accomplish for you to consider me recovered?

- Do you accept my insurance? Do you charge for cancellations?

- What days and hours are you available for appointments? Can I call you between appointments, and if so, is there a charge for that?

better to say something in a clumsy way than to remain silent, waiting for the perfect words to come into your head. Similarly, it is better to bring up the subject yourself rather than waiting for her to mention it or for the best possible moment, although you should try to do it at a time when your friend is calm and not in a hurry to be somewhere or to finish something. Other tips for getting a friend to talk about her eating disorder include the following:

⊙ Be ready to give your friend factual information about bulimia. It may help to have this book with you; offer to lend it to her.

⊙ Avoid attacking or accusing. Use "I" statements instead of "you" statements; for example, "I've noticed that you seem to throw up a lot. Is there something wrong?" instead of "You throw up all the time, so obviously you are bulimic."

⊙ Practice "empathic listening." That means listening with just one intention: to understand what your friend is telling you and how she seems to feel about it. Many people make the mistake of using the time while the other person is talking to think about what they want to say next. The problem with that is that when you're thinking your own thoughts, you can't really pay attention to what your friend is saying! Another element of empathic listening is validating your friend's words and feelings. You can do this by making eye contact, using your body language to show that you are paying attention, responding with small, encouraging words such as "Uh huh" or "I see" or "Tell me more," and resisting the urge to compare yourself to her or talk about similar problems of your own.

⊙ Be ready for rejection. Your friend may not be ready to accept help or to face the reality of her problem. She may even react with denial or anger. Try not to take these reactions personally; remember that your friend is suffering a great deal of emotional pain, and she may lash out at you for raising the subject, but she isn't really angry with you. Give her time and eventually she may be able to talk to you about it.

⊙ Finally, offer to help in any way you can, but don't promise to keep it a secret if she refuses to tell a trusted adult. Tell her how dangerous bulimia is to her health, and tell her that you care about her and want to help her help herself. Tell her that you are always willing to listen and that she should feel free to talk to you any time about her eating disorder or any other problem. Reassure her that you will still be her friend regardless of what she does about her problem.

HOW CAN I TELL IF MY FRIEND HAS BULIMIA?

Bulimia can be very difficult to detect in others, because the bulimic usually feels ashamed of her problem and will go to great lengths to hide it from others. However, there are some signs that you may be able to pick up on if you pay close attention. First, review the questions in the box starting on page 44 entitled How Can I Tell If I Have Bulimia? and apply them to your friend. Then ask yourself:

⊙ Does she seem to be spending more time alone lately?

⊙ Does she frequently go to the bathroom after a meal?

⊙ Have I ever heard her throwing up?

⊙ Have I ever noticed pills in her purse or bedroom?

⊙ Does she have any physical signs such as cuts on her hands or puffy cheeks?

⊙ How often do I see her eat? Does she finish her meals?

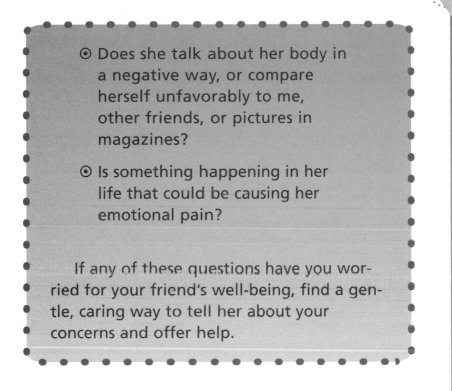

⊙ Does she talk about her body in a negative way, or compare herself unfavorably to me, other friends, or pictures in magazines?

⊙ Is something happening in her life that could be causing her emotional pain?

If any of these questions have you worried for your friend's well-being, find a gentle, caring way to tell her about your concerns and offer help.

4 Don't Go Along with Society's Mistakes

In its June 3, 1996, cover story, entitled "Mission Impossible," *People* magazine addressed the issue of unrealistic body image in Hollywood and how it affects normal Americans. Karen S. Schneider wrote, "In the moral order of today's media-driven universe, the definition of what constitutes beauty or even an acceptable body seems to become more inaccessible every year. The result? Increasingly bombarded by countless 'perfect' body images projected by TV, movies and magazines, many Americans are feeling worse and worse about the workaday bodies they actually inhabit. The people being hurt most are the ones who are most vulnerable: adolescents."

Even if you don't suffer from disordered eating and you don't know anyone who does (which is very unlikely, by the way), there are still things you can do to steer others away from trouble. The way you treat others, from friends and family to strangers and even people you don't like, can

68

LIGHT A CANDLE

If you have lost someone to an eating disorder, visit the Something Fishy Web site on Eating Disorders at:
www.something-fishy.org
and post a tribute to your loved one in the "In Loving Memory" section. Dozens of personal stories appear there, contributed by broken-hearted friends and relatives of eating disorder victims whose bodies could not withstand the effects of their disease.

have a huge impact on their self-esteem. One casual remark about a person's weight or appearance can be the beginning of disordered eating for that person. Before reading this book, you may not have realized how important it is to pay attention to your eating and exercise habits and to watch out for signs of disordered eating and negative body image in yourself and your friends. Now that you know those things, you can begin to apply that knowledge to your treatment of everyone else in your life, from casual acquaintances to strangers. It is time to change our society's impossible ideal of physical beauty, but that won't happen unless people begin to speak and act out against it.

HOW SOCIETY SEES . . .
KAREN CARPENTER

Children and teens today are too young to remember Karen Carpenter, who died in 1983 of a heart attack brought on by her struggle with anorexia and bulimia. She had abused ipecac syrup for years, and became progressively thinner and weaker before beginning treatment. Ironically, she seemed to be on the road to recovery when she died; despite her efforts to help herself, her body was simply too damaged to go on.

Karen is remembered as a talented singer and musician whose death was a needless tragedy. Her weight most likely had no bearing on what her admirers thought of her during her life, and it has nothing to do with the fact that her music has lived on after her death, even attracting a new generation of listeners. Most important, her physical appearance had nothing to do with her talent—it did not improve it or detract from it—but it was the focus of the eating disorders that ultimately stole that talent from the world.

IF YOU AREN'T PART OF THE SOLUTION, YOU'RE PART OF THE PROBLEM

Following are some ways you can work toward changing society's unhealthy obsession with thinness:

- ⊙ Never tease anyone about his or her weight or appearance. You know how painful it can be, so don't do it to someone else, even if that person has been mean to you. Don't make disparaging remarks about a person's looks behind his or her back either; your words may get back to the other person, but even if they don't, you've sent a strong message about intolerance of others to the people with whom you were talking. Some people now refer to such discrimination as "looksism," considering it as offensive and wrong as racism or sexism.

- ⊙ Don't participate in "fat talk" or body hatred. It may seem like the thing to do when all the other girls are complaining about their bodies, and you may even think it would sound stuck-up or arrogant to say that you like your body the way it is, but positive self-talk is not the same as bragging. When you speak positively about yourself, you affirm that you are okay as you are, and that you are no better or worse than anyone else. If your friends think it's wrong of you to like yourself the way you are, they need to learn about building up their own positive self-images. You can try to help them, but if they reject you or make fun of you for it, you need to realize that they are not positive people and are not good influences in your life.

⊙ Consistently remind yourself and others that media images of tiny models are neither realistic nor desirable. Point out to yourself, your family, and your friends that if a real five-foot-eight-inch-tall woman had the same proportions as a Barbie doll, her chest would measure thirty-four inches, her waist would be a miniscule sixteen inches, and her hips would measure twenty-nine inches; she would have an unhealthy twelve percent body-fat ratio, her head would be much too big for her body, and the exaggerated length and shape of her legs would make it impossible for her to walk!

⊙ Be aware of the attitude you project to children, for example, younger siblings or children you baby-sit. Never force them to eat something or to "clean their plates." Do not use food as a reward or take it away as a punishment. If your parents or other adults in your life do this, show them this book and ask them to stop.

⊙ Pay attention to and challenge the messages that media and advertising are sending. If you spot inconsistencies such as an article about self-esteem sandwiched between ads featuring impossibly perfect women, or if your favorite magazine uses only ultra-thin models, write a letter to the editors encouraging them to celebrate diversity by using realistic models. As a consumer, you have power—you're the one who chooses how to spend your money. Don't pay for anything you find offensive, insulting, degrading, or negative.

⊙ If you have a fight with someone, don't give in to the temptation to call her a name that insults her appearance. Those phrases may automatically come out of your mouth when you're mad at someone, and that may even be the only time you use them. Why do so many people reserve "fat cow," "lard ass," and "ugly bitch" for when they're angry? Because they know instinctively that such words are powerful ammunition and cause great pain; people don't say them unless they really want to hurt another person. But now you know that if another girl bumps into you in the hall or even steals your boyfriend, that does not give you the right to say something that could lead to her death.

"LOOKSISM": THE NEWEST CATEGORY OF DISCRIMINATION

If you were to research the history of stand-up comedy through the last century, you would get a good idea of how our society has identified and condemned certain forms of discrimination over the years. If you listen to a typical comedian today, you are unlikely to hear jokes that put down a particular race or ethnicity. You almost certainly won't hear jokes about handicapped people, and only comedians with very poor taste joke about homosexuals or abused women anymore. What you probably will hear, however, are jokes that make fun of people for the way they look. Some comedians even interact with their audiences by insulting people in the front row, calling the men ugly and the women fat. This category of put-downs now has a name: looksism, or discriminating against someone based on his or her looks. It used to be thought of as harmless fun, but now that we are beginning to see how much damage such remarks can do, there is hope that looksism will someday be considered as offensive as every other form of discrimination. But as long as people continue to laugh at these remarks, comedians will continue to say them. We will be able to tell that progress against looksism has been made when comedians no longer make fun of a person's appearance because they know no one will laugh.

As you continue to become aware of the ways in which different people are perceived, you will notice more and more that celebrities are expected to be perfect and are often very harshly criticized if they don't live up to that ideal. Ironically, they are also ridiculed for being shallow or self-centered or vain when they refuse to wear anything but designer clothes or they subject themselves to plastic surgery. Why do we make it clear that we expect perfection from these people, but then laugh at them when they try to achieve it? The boxed personality profiles throughout this book, entitled "How Society Sees . . . ," give insight into how this phenomenon has affected some famous people.

5 Other Eating Disorders and Related Conditions

The American Anorexia/Bulimia Association reports that approximately 15 percent of young women have "substantially disordered eating attitudes and behaviors" and more than five million Americans are struggling with eating disorders. Of that number, some are bulimic, while others are anorexic or suffer from binge-eating disorder (BED). Beyond the three most serious eating disorders, however, are a number of other conditions, including compulsive exercise, malnutrition, fad or yo-yo dieting, smoking, alcohol and drug abuse, depression, and even self-mutilation and obsessive-compulsive disorder (OCD), which are correlated in varying degrees with disordered eating.

COMPULSIVE EXERCISE

Compulsive exercise has long been considered a side effect of anorexia or bulimia, but researchers are now beginning to think of it as a separate problem that may occur on its own and often accompanies another eating disorder. Since everyone knows that exercise burns calories, it makes sense that people who are obsessed with thinness would use exercise to lose weight. But how can you tell whether your exercise regimen is healthy or compulsive?

Tabitha sticks to a strict exercise program, making sure to work through two aerobics tapes before dinner and another before bed. This sometimes cuts into her homework time, but she figures keeping herself in shape is more important.

Charlene's volleyball coach told her that she needs to work on her reaction time and her vertical leaps, so she spends two hours each afternoon in the back yard, jumping up to touch the mark she made on the garage, and whenever she can she gets friends or teammates to come over and practice with her.

Calvin wants to make the golf team next year, so he hits practice balls into a net in his yard until dark every night. He never realized golf could be such a good workout, but by the time he's finished his shirt is soaked with sweat and his shoulder muscles ache. He figures with all this work he'll have no problem making the team.

Are these people healthy fitness fans, or compulsive exercisers? What choices are they making about exercise that affect other important facets of their lives? Tabitha's belief that keeping herself in shape is more important than homework could be a sign that she has slipped from a healthy interest in fitness into an unhealthy addiction. Then again, Tabitha may be overweight and committed to losing just enough to bring herself to a healthy level. Charlene's and Calvin's stories are also not clear-cut; they may be dedicated athletes destined for greatness, or they may be exercise addicts who don't know how to keep their workout routines from dominating their lives.

If you exercise regularly or participate in a sport, ask yourself why you do it. Is it because you enjoy the activity, because you like to win, or because you know that exercise is an important component of overall health? Is it more than that? If you quit your team or skipped your workouts for a while, how would you feel about yourself? If your self-esteem is based largely on your performance in a sport or in your ability to stick to a workout regimen, you may be headed for a problem with exercise compulsion.

MALNUTRITION

Most people think of malnutrition as a chronic condition affecting only poverty-stricken children in other countries, where there isn't enough food, or even water, for everyone. The fact is that malnutrition exists in America, even among people who can have all the food they want. In cases of child abuse and neglect, it is not uncommon to find that the victims have not been fed properly; they may be low on certain vitamins and minerals or they may be so starved that their bellies are swollen like those of the children in the pictures we all see from impoverished third world countries. However, many children with loving parents are lacking in vitamins and minerals crucial for health and growth, including calcium and iron. The reason for this is poor eating habits.

A child who always drinks pop instead of milk will almost certainly develop a calcium deficiency. A child, especially a girl, who is allowed to eat no red meat but is not taught how to get the iron she needs from other food sources will probably become anemic. These are common, completely preventable forms of malnutrition in this country. Among older children and even adults, fad dieting can also lead to malnutrition. Any diet that severely limits or forbids the consumption of an entire food group, such as carbohydrates or fats, puts the dieter in danger of missing out on important nutrients, either because they are found mostly in the forbidden foods, or because they come from allowable foods but cannot be absorbed by the body without the help of the forbidden foods.

Besides depriving your body of important nutrients, which in some cases cannot be replaced simply by taking a daily multivitamin, limiting yourself to a strict diet regimen that does not include any of your favorite foods can backfire. The lack of certain foods, such as fats, combined with the psychological strain of harsh dieting, can bring on a binge in which you "lose control" and eat everything you've been forcing yourself to avoid. The subsequent guilt that you feel after the binge then prompts you to go back on the same, or an even stricter, diet. This cycle of impossible dieting and loss of control is called "yo-yo dieting," and it is bad for your health; besides putting you at risk for malnutrition, it could lead to an eating disorder.

It is important that every child learn about the body's nutritional requirements and think about them with every meal and snack. A child who understands that drinking pop, eating candy, skipping meals, or avoiding entire food groups all the time is damaging to his or her health will be more likely to make better choices. If you recognize these or similar poor eating habits in yourself, do some research on nutrition and begin to make healthy changes in the way you eat. If you don't get well-balanced meals at home, list some healthy meals and foods and ask the person who prepares your meals to make them for you. It is never too late to learn about nutrition and to begin to provide your body with the proper fuel.

SMOKING AND SUBSTANCE ABUSE

Any foreign substance that you put into your body alters it in some way. Tobacco, alcohol, and all drugs and supplements have various effects on your brain, heart, lungs, kidneys, liver, or other organs, and also on your body's respiratory, circulatory, endocrine, and digestive systems. Medications are used to make you better if you're sick by bringing on good changes in your body's organs and systems, and supplements are intended to help your body reach its highest health potential. You have probably heard about the negative effects that smoking, drinking, and using drugs can have on your body, but did you know that they can also contribute to disordered eating?

Many people believe that smoking can make you lose weight, so many girls use cigarettes as a dieting tool. This is extremely dangerous to your health, and it doesn't even work! The reason some people lose

HOW SOCIETY SEES . . . MARILYN MONROE

Marilyn Monroe was the embodiment of physical perfection in her day, but by today's standards she would be considered overweight and out of shape. She would wear a size fourteen, making her an average-size woman. The star of movies including *Some Like It Hot, Gentlemen Prefer Blondes,* and *The Seven-Year Itch,* Marilyn made headlines with her controversial lifestyle. Her sexy image drew nonstop rumors of scandal, including whisperings of an affair with President John F. Kennedy, and her mysterious death is still the subject of conspiracy theories.

Yet some people saw through the Marilyn Monroe image to the young woman behind it: Norma Jeane Mortensen, an illegitimate child born to a family with a severe history of mental illness and placed in foster care when her mother was committed to a mental institution. In his song "Candle in the Wind," Elton John paid tribute to Marilyn's efforts to remain true to herself despite the attempts of people hoping to influence her for their purposes. He compared her to a "candle in the wind, never knowing who to cling to when the rain set in."

In an interview a week before her death in 1962, Marilyn expressed her frustration at the image that she was expected to uphold: "That's the trouble—a sex symbol becomes a thing. I just hate being a thing." No one has determined whether her death was a suicide, an accident, or murder, but in any case, if Marilyn had had an effective network of supportive, positive people in her life, her death might have been averted.

weight when they start smoking is that they tend to replace snacks with cigarettes. The reason some people gain weight when they quit smoking is just the opposite: instead of "consuming" a cigarette, they reach for a snack. If you teach yourself to find something else to do with your hands and mouth instead of smoking or overeating—for example, a hobby such as singing or drawing, or an activity that you can't do while smoking or eating, such as a sport—you can avoid two health risks, smoking and overeating, at the same time.

Drinking alcohol lowers your inhibitions and your ability to make good choices. Alcohol is high in calories, and when people drink they also tend to eat more than normal. So, besides being dangerous to your health and your safety, not to mention illegal if you're underage, drinking can lead to binge eating. Chronic and persistent consumption of alcohol (alcoholism) can also lead to malnutrition.

Many drugs have some of the same effects as alcohol: They lower your inhibitions, make you feel superconfident or invincible, or make you forget all the reasons you have for eating healthily. Some drugs also increase or decrease your appetite. Laxatives, which are supposed to be used when you have constipation and can't have a bowel movement, and diuretics, which force your body to rid itself of water, are both commonly abused by people with eating disorders. Syrup of ipecac, which is intended to be used only to induce vomiting in people who have ingested poisons, is a poison itself and can cause death when misused. In fact, singer Karen Carpenter's death has been attributed to abuse of ipecac. The use of any drug for a purpose other than the one listed on the label can be extremely dangerous. No drug should be used to lose weight or to purge excess calories. The only exception to this rule is the use of a prescription drug, prescribed for you (not for a friend or parent) by a doctor and used under that doctor's close supervision. Even then, drug use should be a last resort for treating a dangerously obese person; a good, responsible doctor will never prescribe a weight-loss drug to a teen who simply wants to look better.

DEPRESSION

Most people who suffer from eating disorders are also suffering to some degree from depression. Defined as an emotional condition characterized by feelings of hopelessness, inadequacy, or self-hatred, depression can be caused by any number of things or by nothing specific. Some people are prone to depression because of a chemical imbalance in their brains, but other people become depressed as a result of a crisis in their lives or because they feel more and more unable to cope with everyday life. Depression does not cause eating disorders, and eating disorders do not cause depression; instead, the circumstances in a person's life that cause one condition can also cause the other. When they occur together, both conditions must be treated in order to bring the sufferer back to a healthy state. The health professional treating a victim of an eating disorder, or depression, or both, may prescribe an antidepressant medication to assist the sufferer in regaining psychological control and equilibrium. When that is accomplished, the person is better able to learn what she needs to change in her life to bring about recovery. It is important to realize that an antidepressant is not a cure; it simply reduces or eliminates the symptoms of depression and allows the sufferer to work on changing the things that brought it on in the first place. In that respect, the sufferer actually cures herself.

SELF-MUTILATION

Some people act on their feelings of self-hatred by actually injuring themselves. But unlike the bulimic, who injures her body by depriving it of nutrients and straining its organs and systems, a person who practices self-mutilation cuts her body with a knife or razor blade; burns herself; pulls out her hair, eyelashes, or eyebrows; or does something else to cause herself pain. She does not consciously intend to commit suicide; instead, her goal is to replace her emotional pain with more tolerable physical pain, to break through her emotional numbness and allow herself to feel something, or to express anger or other painful feelings.

People who practice self-mutilation are also often suffering from an eating disorder. The thing that self-mutilators have in common with bulimics, anorexics, binge eaters, alcoholics, and drug abusers is that they are attempting to rid themselves of psychological pain.

OBSESSIVE-COMPULSIVE DISORDER

Obsessive-compulsive disorder, or OCD, is a serious psychological condition characterized by rigid adherence to rituals, such as checking door locks ten times each night or washing hands after touching anything or anyone (sometimes dozens of times each day). Jack Nicholson's character in the movie *As Good as It Gets* suffered from OCD, and he had rituals for locking doors, putting on his shoes, washing his hands, avoiding sidewalk cracks, and many other common elements of daily life. When he was forced to deviate from these rituals, he experienced great psychological distress—fear, confusion, and desperation to return his life to "normal."

Rituals are also common among eating disorder sufferers. Something as simple as refusing to eat any food that has touched another food on your plate, or insisting on eating one food at a time in a particular order (for example, the potatoes first, then the meat, then the vegetable) may signal an

HOW SOCIETY SEES . . . ALICIA SILVERSTONE

Alicia Silverstone was first noticed in an Aerosmith music video and became famous for the perfectly fashionable, perfectly thin character she portrayed in 1995's *Clueless*. Yet, as she prepared to star as Batgirl in *Batman and Robin* (1997), Alicia became the target of criticism more severe and cruel than even the trashiest tabloids usually produce. The reason for this public outcry and condemnation of a nineteen-year-old actress? She had gained weight. In an article challenging Hollywood's—and, by extension, America's—unrealistic standard of beauty, *People* magazine reporter Karen S. Schneider noted that at the March 1996 Academy Awards, Alicia "did the unthinkable: She appeared in public despite the fact that, like many of her teenage peers around the country, she had just added on five or ten pounds."

"Was she congratulated for the self-confidence and assurance it took to be herself?" Schneider continued. "Hardly. The tabloids . . . blared out lines like

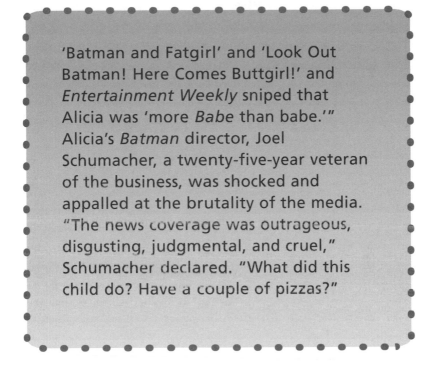

'Batman and Fatgirl' and 'Look Out Batman! Here Comes Buttgirl!' and *Entertainment Weekly* sniped that Alicia was 'more *Babe* than babe.'" Alicia's *Batman* director, Joel Schumacher, a twenty-five-year veteran of the business, was shocked and appalled at the brutality of the media. "The news coverage was outrageous, disgusting, judgmental, and cruel," Schumacher declared. "What did this child do? Have a couple of pizzas?"

unhealthy preoccupation with eating. Such rituals do not automatically indicate that the person who follows them is suffering from OCD, but it could mean that the person has an underlying problem that is causing her to seek comfort in rigidly pre-scribed routines.

6 Your Health: A Reality Check

Do you think you need to lose weight? Wait—don't say yes. Not yet, anyway. You may be completely convinced that you are overweight, but you may be wrong. Promise yourself that you will read this entire chapter before deciding. That way, if you are at an acceptable weight, you can begin to explore the reasons you were so sure you needed to reduce. Are you suffering from low self-esteem or negative body image? If after learning about the facts and fallacies of body weight, body-fat percentage, fitness level, and nutrition, you determine that some weight loss would be a good idea for you, you can begin armed with the facts and build a sane, safe plan for gradually reducing your weight and allowing your body to be its strongest, fittest, and healthiest ever.

WHAT DO YOU SEE IN THE MIRROR?

You probably think you know yourself pretty well. You're painfully aware of every pimple, and you just know everyone is staring at the run in your panty-hose. Every time someone remarks on your appearance, you don't doubt what they say because, well, they have eyes, they can see you, so they must be right, right?

Flipping through an old photo album, a young woman came across a picture of herself in elementary school. She winced slightly at the image—the dorky haircut, the pasty complexion—and remembered how awkward she had felt back then. The boys had always called her fat, but looking at this picture, she thought, "I don't look fat here. . . ." There were other kids in the picture, and she began mentally identifying each of them, her classmates from fifth grade. But while scanning the familiar faces, the woman noticed something she had never seen before: these kids all looked so SHORT! None of them was any taller than her shoulder. With a jolt, she realized that no one had ever called her tall, just fat; now it was plain to see that she had indeed been much bigger than everyone else back then, but not overweight. Awestruck at this revelation, the woman thought back to all the times she had been wounded by the other kids' words—and all along they had been wrong!

You may find it hard to believe, but what you see in the mirror may not be what's really there. It is crucial that you learn to see yourself as you really are; then you can make an accurate assessment of your strengths and weaknesses and learn to love yourself as you are, not as society wants you to be.

What you see when you step on the scale is not a good representation of what you really are either. That number is just one factor in a long list of factors that together show you the "big picture" of your overall health and fitness. Unfortunately, most Americans obsess over their weight, determining much of their self-image and self-esteem from the judgment of the scale. This is neither healthy nor accurate. A realistic assessment of your physical health must include not only your weight, but also your frame size, your body-fat percentage, your nutritional habits, and your performance in various tests of physical fitness.

WHAT DOES WEIGHT INDICATE?

When you step on a scale, it tells you how much your body weighs. When you stand in front of a height chart, it tells you how tall you are. These functions seem pretty similar—they both give you factual information about your body, and each can be compared to past measurements to track changes in your body's growth. If these measurements have so much in common, why is it that most people pay little attention to their height, but almost everyone freaks out about their weight?

My class took a field trip to the science center, and they had this machine that tells you your weight on the moon. A couple kids tried it, but then someone figured out how to calculate your real weight based on your moon weight, and suddenly no one wanted to try it any more.

Every time I see one of those "guess-your-weight" guys at a carnival, I am amazed that some people will actually do it. I mean, how can they stand having their weight announced in front of a crowd? I don't care how many cute little teddy bears I could win, I would never step on a scale in public!

Many people are very secretive about their weight. Even into adulthood, many women refuse to reveal their weight or to be weighed at a doctor's office. This can cause serious problems when a woman needs surgery, because the anesthesiologist uses your weight to determine how much anesthesia to give you. If you say you weigh less than you do, you could wake up in the middle of the surgery!

It's time to realize that weight is just a number, like blood pressure and pulse and height and respiration rate, which provides some information about your body but does not give the whole picture of your health. It also does not correspond to your clothing size. Most important, it does not tell you how much fat you have in your body—it tells you the combined weight of all the water, bone, muscle, blood, and everything else, including fat, in your body, and that's certainly not a good measurement of your fitness, let alone of your worth as a person.

When a person is described as overweight, what is really meant is that the person is overfat. This may not be true, however; many, many people do not fit into the ideal category for their height and frame size on those height/weight charts that doctors and life insurance companies use, and they are not necessarily overfat. Muscle weighs more than fat, so people who have a lot of muscle mass will weigh more than people of the same height and frame size who have less muscle mass. That does not mean that the person who weighs less is healthier—probably the opposite, in fact.

Some people also weigh more or less than the average for their height due to their frame size. There are several ways of measuring your frame size; some doctors simply look at your fingers, but there are charts that can tell you whether you have a small, average, or large frame based on your wrist measurement or other measurements. In general, if your hands and feet are larger than those of others your age and gender, and if your wrists and ankles are bigger around, you probably have a large frame—what some people call "big-boned," an expression that used to be an excuse for being overweight, but some people really do have bigger bones than others.

So how can you tell whether you are overfat? One popular cereal company used to promote its low-calorie product as a weight-loss tool and advised consumers that if they could "pinch an inch" around their waists, they needed to start eating this cereal. Besides that old technique, there are many tools and methods for measuring body fat, many of which are available through your doctor's office or from your gym teacher or coach. Before you use one, however, do

Muscle weighs more than fat, so people who have a lot of muscle mass will weigh more than people of the same height and frame size who have less muscle mass. That does not mean that the person who weighs less is healthier—probably the opposite, in fact.

some research and learn about the many ways, some accurate and some not, some expensive and some not, to calculate body-fat percentage. Check out the information on the skin caliper test (it's not painful, although it sounds as if it could be!), the body mass index, and even the fancy underwater and ultrasound methods.

Even if you do find that you are overfat, don't skip the rest of this chapter! It is possible to have a good fitness level and still carry some extra weight, so simply learning that your body-fat percentage is more than it should be does not give you an accurate idea of your overall health and fitness. Also, if you discover that you have a healthy percentage of body fat, you should still assess your nutritional and exercise habits to see if there are areas in which you can improve. Just being in the right category of leanness does not automatically make you healthy and fit. So, keep reading!

ARE YOU A COUCH POTATO, OR FIT AS A FIDDLE?

Ask anyone who works in the health and fitness field for their opinion of what constitutes an ideal fitness level, and you are likely to get an animated response. The subject of fitness, including what it is exactly, how to measure it, and how to determine your level of it, is controversial and open to broad interpretation. Much research has been and continues to be conducted in this area, but there is no single, definitive test to measure every person's fitness level. Some of the factors to consider when assessing your fitness level include:

⊙ **Cardiovascular fitness.** If you are a runner, you most likely have good cardiovascular health, because running is an aerobic activity that strengthens your heart and improves your endurance. If you get out of breath from running a short distance or from climbing a flight of stairs, your "aerobic capacity" is probably not very high, or you may have asthma or another pulmonary, or breathing, disease.

⊙ **Flexibility**. The range of motion through which you are able to move your muscles is your flexibility level. If you are a dancer or cheerleader, you are likely to be quite flexible. It is interesting to note that many people who are naturally very flexible do not have very high muscle strength, and those whose overall strength is high tend to be relatively inflexible, or "muscle-bound." This is simply because strong muscles are not as easy to stretch. There is no reason you can't be both strong and flexible, however—you must simply remember to emphasize both strength training and stretching in your exercise routine.

⊙ **Strength.** If you are a gymnast, you probably have a great deal of strength from constantly lifting your own body weight. Similarly, figure skaters tend to have very strong lower bodies, and swimmers' arm and shoulder muscles are usually well developed. If your workout emphasizes strength-building exercises, it is important for you to work on flexibility as well to prevent injury and allow your muscles to reach their full potential. It is also important to know that while, on average, males tend to have higher muscle strength than females because of the hormonal, body size, and muscle mass differences of the two genders, there is no reason that a female cannot be strong enough to participate in any sport or activity she chooses.

⊙ **Agility.** This component of fitness measures your coordination and ability to move and change direction quickly. A running back in football is an example of someone who must exhibit a high level of agility—if not, he'll be squashed by the defensemen on a regular basis! Tennis players, boxers, and basketball players also must be quick and light on their feet.

So how can you tell how strong, flexible, agile, and cardiovascularly fit you are? If you are involved in a sport, you probably already have some idea of your fitness in each category based on your performance compared to your teammates' and on your coach's assessment. If you do not participate in an

HOW SOCIETY SEES . . . PAMELA ANDERSON LEE

Pamela Anderson Lee became famous in her role as lifeguard C. J. Parker on *Baywatch*, a television show which, thanks mostly to her, is frequently called "Babewatch." Reported to wear a size two dress and a double-D bra, she is to many people a physically perfect woman: impossibly thin, yet gloriously chesty (thanks to breast implants, which she recently had removed), with perfect hair, perfect teeth, perfect nails, and a perfect face. Her public persona in interviews on late-night TV and talk shows is that of a loving mother to her two sons and an all-around nice person. With so much going for her, news of her victimization as an abused wife came as quite a shock.

In her early days on *Baywatch*, she used the name Pamela Sue Anderson, later dropping her middle name to become known simply as Pamela Anderson. When she married Mötley Crüe rocker Tommy Lee, she became Pamela Anderson Lee, and then when they split up in 1998, some people began to refer to her again as Pamela Anderson. But dropping Tommy

Lee's name, if she chooses to, won't erase the pain of her abusive marriage. Despite her seemingly perfect life, a perception that was based on the apparent perfection of her body, Pamela was not immune to one of the most serious health risks a woman can face: beatings at the hands of her husband, the person who was supposed to love and respect her above all others. Her sad situation should serve as proof that no amount of makeup, toning, dieting, or plastic surgery will guarantee happiness.

organized sport, your physical education class may give you some idea of how fit you are. Your gym teacher can help you to gauge your fitness by critiquing your performance in class; he or she may also be able to provide some simple tests to do on your own. Another way to evaluate your fitness level is by paying attention to how your body reacts to the activities in your everyday life, such as climbing stairs, running for a bus, walking home from school or to a friend's house, and playing at recess or outside of school. Some points to consider:

⊙ How good are you at catching a ball or a Frisbee? Are you able to throw it back all the way to the other person?

⊙ Can you bend over and touch your toes without bending your knees? Can you reach farther and lay your palms flat on the ground?

⊙ Do you enjoy activities that test your balance, like playing "Twister" or standing on your head?

⊙ When you climb a set of stairs, how far can you get before you're out of breath? Do you run up each flight, or do you stop on the landings to catch your breath?

⊙ Can you keep up with the others when you play football, basketball, or tag? Do you feel as if they aren't moving fast enough?

⊙ How fast can you run around the bases in a game of baseball or softball? How often do you get tagged out?

⊙ When you hurry through the mall or home from school, do your parents or friends have to slow down for you, or do you slow down for them?

When you stop to think about these things, you should end up with an idea of how you compare to your friends, teammates, or family members. While this is not a scientific way of measuring your fitness and could be influenced by a number of factors—for example, if you hang out with members of the track team but you're not a runner, or if you have asthma or another health problem that limits your physical stamina—it gives you a place to begin thinking about how fit you actually are.

If you discover that you are almost always the one left behind when the other kids take off running, or you find yourself saying "wait up" a lot, you may need to improve your cardiovascular fitness. If you can't touch your toes, you may need to work on flexibility. If people tease you for being clumsy, perhaps some agility exercises would help. And if you have trouble lifting a bag full of school books or helping your parents with housework or gardening, some push-ups, leg lifts, and abdominal crunches, done correctly, may be just what you need.

If you think a health problem may be keeping you from achieving your fitness potential, talk to your family doctor. In the past, people with asthma or other conditions worsened by exercise were discouraged from physical activity, but health experts today know that everyone needs some exercise to stay healthy. There are treatments that will allow you to exercise and participate in sports safely, and you may find that, without having to worry about how exercising will affect your health condition, you may get a lot more enjoyment from working out.

Most important, remember that your fitness level does not measure your intelligence, your willpower, or your goodness as a person. It is simply a snapshot of one aspect of your overall health, and it is something you can change. If you choose to embark on a program to improve your fitness, make sure you're doing it to improve your health and to please yourself, not to try to make yourself perfect or popular or to make your parents happy.

IF "YOU ARE WHAT YOU EAT," DOES THAT MAKE ME A COOKIE?

The "facts" of nutrition are constantly changing. One year fat is forbidden, the next year it's carbohydrates. Researchers battle over the nutritional value of nuts (is that good fat or bad fat?), eggs (cholesterol!), citrus fruits (packed with vitamins, but are they too acidic?), and various obscure vegetables (what is arugula, anyway?). Alarming reports on cancer-fighting and cancer-causing compounds in foods make the news every day, and new miracle weight-loss methods are always in the spotlight. People spend millions of dollars a year on supplements and devices that claim to provide maximum nutrition, cancer protection, and weight loss, with minimal effort in no time flat.

It's enough to make you lose your appetite—or your ability to control what you eat. Unfortunately, all the confusion surrounding good nutrition makes it even harder to avoid disordered eating. Our society's fixation with physical perfection is what fuels the nutrition craze, and it leads to overwhelming pressure never to eat anything "bad" and never to eat one calorie more than you should. The constant anxiety over every bite you take makes it very difficult, and for some people seemingly impossible, to develop a simple, sensible, stress-free approach to eating.

STAR-POWERED SELF-ESTEEM

Tennis superstar Monica Seles refuses to be a slave to the bathroom scale. She summarizes her healthy philosophy on weight with this thought: "As long as I'm able to move and feel good, it doesn't matter."

Fighting your way through the jungle of information and misinformation on what to eat (and how much, and when) may seem like more trouble than it's worth, but with a few basic guidelines you can weed out the junk and learn what you need to know to build an optimal eating plan for yourself. But first you need to see where you are now. Below we'll consider your eating schedule and then what you actually eat.

DO YOU GET YOUR THREE SQUARES A DAY?

"Three square meals a day" used to be the way to go. As long as you got a good breakfast, lunch, and dinner, you could rest assured that you were giving your body the best possible nutrition. While it's not the only consideration anymore, eating at least three meals a day is still an important guideline.

New research has confirmed what many parents and educators already suspected: Children who eat breakfast learn more easily. If you start the day with some sort of food, you are likely to do better in school. Your breakfast doesn't have to be traditional breakfast food, either—a piece of leftover pizza is better than nothing at all. Lunch is also important, but unlike breakfast, which you can eat at home, your lunch is subject to the scrutiny of your friends, and that makes getting a healthful, well-balanced midday meal even more challenging. Dinner is important not just for its nutritional content but as a family event as well. Some people also need a snack between meals to keep their energy up.

Do you regularly eat something for breakfast,

lunch, and dinner? If not, how do you feel? Are you starving by lunchtime, or sleepy in the afternoon? Are you so hungry by the time you get home from school that you scarf down anything you can find?

IS YOUR NUTRITION A PYRAMID—OR JUST A SHAPELESS MASS?

You've heard of the "four basic food groups," but what about the U.S. Department of Agriculture's Food Guide Pyramid? Many brands of bread, cereal, and other foods have the pyramid on their labels. The pyramid shape makes it easy to see which foods you should eat more of (the base of the pyramid) and which you should choose less often (the ones at the tip), and the groupings not only expand on the "four basics" but also provide the number of servings you should eat of each.

Depending on your weight, age, and energy needs, the Food Guide Pyramid recommends eating six to eleven servings of bread, cereal, rice, or pasta; three to five servings of vegetables; two to four servings of fruits; two to three servings of milk, yogurt, or cheese; and two to three servings of meat, poultry, fish, dry beans, eggs, or nuts every day. Fats, oils, and sweets appear at the tip of the pyramid with the suggestion that they be used "sparingly." You need to do a little detective work to learn exactly what a "serving" is; read the labels on your favorite foods and you may be surprised to discover that a single serving is smaller than you thought.

The Food Guide Pyramid is not the whole story, however. You should read up on balanced nutrition and educate yourself about the effects that proteins, carbohydrates, and fats as well as vitamins, minerals, and fiber have on your body and the reasons that you need some of each. Be suspicious of any diet plan that recommends eliminating an entire category of food. You should also learn how to determine how many calories you need in a day and how to track your daily intake without becoming obsessed with counting calories and measuring portions. Remember, balance is the key, in what you eat and in how you perceive and react to food.

How do your eating habits compare to the Food Guide Pyramid's recommendations? Do you eat some fruits and vegetables every day? If not, why not? If you don't like the taste or texture of certain fruits and veggies, experiment with new ones or with new ways of preparing them until you find something you like.

ARE SNACKS AND DESSERTS REALLY EVIL?

One of the first things most people do when they "go on a diet" is eliminate snacks and desserts. This may seem like a healthy choice, but it's really not. In fact, most cases of anorexia begin as diets, and most of those diets begin with cutting various food groups and categories. It is normal to like foods that are very sweet or very salty, and there is nothing wrong with eating them occasionally. The important thing is making sure that your nutritional needs are met first. For example, if you feel hungry a few hours after dinner and are debating between having an apple and having a few cookies, think back on what you've eaten that day: if you haven't had any fruit, you should choose the apple, but if you have already eaten the recommended number of serv- ings of fruit, the cookies might be okay.

Another important factor to consider is your individual energy needs. Your body may not be able to handle just three meals a day; you may need to have a snack in between to keep you going. Contrary to what the commercials say, however, a candy bar with nuts, caramel, and chocolate is not a healthful snack, and neither is a can of pop! A handful of plain peanuts, some raisins, and a glass of milk is a much better nutritional value and will help your body to maintain a steady blood sugar level, avoiding the energy spikes and crashes caused by a big dose of sugar.

Dessert after dinner is also not necessarily bad. It depends on what it is and how much of it you eat. Americans are quite accustomed to finishing a meal with something sweet; fruit can satisfy your sweet tooth without packing in too many empty calories. There are many delicious recipes for fruit- based desserts, including low-sugar apple pie or poached pears with raisins—check out some cook- books for alternatives to the same old ice cream and cake!

So, how much sugar do you eat in a day? Chances are it's more than you should, and that it's hidden in foods you would never suspect. Most Americans, especially children and teens, consume far more sugar than their bodies need. Much of this imbalance can be attributed to media images of sweet snacks that give you energy and are lots of fun to eat—or so they tell us. These images make you think that the sugary snack they are promoting

IS IT HEALTHY TO BE A VEGETARIAN?

There is one diet variation that eliminates food categories but can be followed in a healthy manner: vegetarianism. Traditionally, being a vegetarian has meant not eating meat, but there are actually quite a number of variations on vegetarianism. Some people simply do not eat beef or other red meats; others avoid all animal products including beef, chicken, pork, and fish and even eggs and dairy products such as milk, cheese, and yogurt; and many people's vegetarian habits fall somewhere between these two extremes. A person's reasons for choosing a vegetarian diet may include religious or political beliefs that forbid eating another creature, or health considerations linked to allergies or animal fats. If you are a vegetarian, it is possible for you to fulfill your nutritional needs, but it takes much more planning and effort and may be more expensive. If you choose a vegetarian lifestyle, make sure you educate yourself and are committed to it for healthy reasons, not for weight loss or because your friends are doing it.

is great and you must try it. It tastes good, so you go back for more. But besides all the candy and treats that we consciously choose to eat, we get much of the excess sugar in our diets as additives in foods that we think are wholesome and healthy— foods like peanut butter, cereal, granola bars, juice, and yogurt. If you read the labels on the foods you eat regularly, you will most likely be amazed at the things that contain added sugar. You can change your eating habits and resist overloading on unneeded sugar; all it takes is knowing how to recognize inaccurate or misleading advertising, being a smart consumer who reads lists of ingredients and product labels, and having a firm desire to give your body the best in nutritional value.

SHOULD I GET A SECOND OPINION?

By now you probably have a pretty good idea of what *you* think your fitness and nutritional levels are, but what if you're still not sure that you are gauging them correctly? Talking to friends is a great way to test your ideas, but make sure the friends you choose to share your thoughts with are supportive, positive people. You don't need anyone giving you bad advice or ridiculing you for working toward a goal as important as improving your health. The same goes for talking to adults. If you seek out the opinion of your gym teacher, coach, counselor, parents, or family doctor, and any of them reacts in an unsupportive or critical way, find someone else to be your fitness mentor. This doesn't mean that they won't tell you negative things— they may say that you do need improvement in certain areas—but it does mean that any feedback you receive will be respectful, kind, and constructive.

SO WHAT DID YOU LEARN?

Now you know that your fitness and nutrition levels are much more important than your weight, and that interpreting what your weight indicates about your overall health is quite difficult. If you have read this entire chapter, answered each of its questions in relation to your body and your exercise and eating habits, have made a sincere effort to evaluate yourself fairly, and you have found that you honestly do need to lose weight, don't panic! You are still the same worthwhile, valuable person you were before you picked up this book, and needing to improve your fitness level does not make you bad, undesirable, ugly, or stupid. Do some more research or talk to your doctor, parents, or someone else you feel comfortable with about changing your eating habits and adding exercise to your life in a reasonable, healthy manner. Develop a plan, begin, begin again if you slip up, and keep at it. Give yourself the same courtesy and support you would give to a friend in your shoes.

Here are a few more tips to help you as you begin to revamp your eating habits:

⊙ Ask the person who buys the groceries in your family to consider your dietary needs; give him or her a list of foods that you want to add to your diet and a list of foods that you don't want to eat—things with no nutritional value.

⊙ Remember that moderation and balance should be your focus. Allow yourself an occasional treat, even if it's nothing but sugary, empty calories, and don't feel guilty about it! It's okay to enjoy your food, and any food, even a candy bar, can have a place in a well-balanced, healthy nutritional plan.

⊙ Instead of practicing an "always/never" mindset, as in "I will always eat fruit and I will never eat dessert," fill your self-talk with "more often": "I eat vegetables more often than I eat pizza; I choose fruit more often than I choose cake." There is no need to deny yourself your favorite foods; that will only discourage you. If your favorites are not high in nutritional value, fit them into your diet once in a while—perhaps once a week, but not every day.

⊙ Learn to resist well-meaning people who push you to eat foods you don't want to eat. If your grandmother always gives you a plate of cookies when you visit her, or if your parents always serve dessert after dinner, explain to them that you appreciate their thoughtfulness but you are trying to improve your eating habits. You might say, "Gram, I sure do love your cookies! But I'm only going to eat one right now because I don't want to spoil my dinner. May I take the rest home?" Then share the cookies with your family or friends. If your family always has dessert along with dinner, have a chat with your mom or dad, perhaps suggesting that they allow each family member to get his or her own dessert later in the evening. That way you can skip dessert if you want to and not have to leave the table early, or worse, be forced to watch everyone else indulge. Remember to state your case in a kind, appreciative manner; a lot of people show their love by offering food and may feel hurt if they perceive that you are rejecting them. If you get this sort of reaction, reassure them that you are grateful for their effort and you love them as much as ever, and you're just trying to be as healthy as you can be. The important thing is that you take control of your eating and don't allow someone else to guilt-trip you into eating something you don't want.

⊙ Remember that the word "diet" does not refer simply to a short-term plan intended to make you lose weight. The way you eat and always have eaten and always will eat is your "diet"; it's not just about losing weight, but about what you choose as fuel for your body. As you begin to make changes in your diet, do so not with the intention of toughing it out for a few months and then going back to your old ways, but instead with the intention of making permanent, positive changes in the way you take care of your body.

⊙ Well-meaning friends or even adults who should know better may offer you bad advice such as various fad diets,or tactics such as meal-skipping. Assess everything before you try it, and discard any advice that sounds dangerous or too good to be true. Be your own best advocate!

Adding exercise to your life may seem like a daunting task, but with a little creative thinking it can be fun and easy. If you are already into sports, the job is half-done: participate in extra practice sessions or with another team, or get a group of teammates together to work with you on improving your skills. For example, if you play softball, find one or two teammates who are willing to stay after practice for some throwing drills. If you swim, get there early and spend an extra ten minutes or so doing laps. If you are starting from scratch, it may seem very strange to get up and get moving, but the hardest part is simply getting started: once you've done that, you can count on momentum and your good feelings to keep you coming back for more.

Following are some pointers for making your exercise routine exciting, fun, and safe:

- ⊙ Find a friend to exercise with. Sometimes promising to work out with someone else will motivate you to do it even if you don't feel like it, and then you'll be glad you did!

- ⊙ Get involved in an activity that has a purpose beyond just burning calories. For example, some people can't stand exercising just for the sake of exercise, so they join a bowling league or take a karate class or find some other way to exercise while learning something or improving a skill.

- ⊙ Build variety into your workouts. Instead of planning to do the same hour-long aerobics tape every day, think of something different for each day of the week. One day you might try a yoga tape, another day you could concentrate on stretching, the next day you might get a one-day pass for the local gym. You could base your choices on the weather, planning to go for a bike ride if it's sunny but spend some time on the treadmill with a good book if it's raining.

- ⊙ Give yourself a break. If you get sick, give yourself time to heal. Don't feel

HOW SOCIETY SEES . . .
KATE WINSLET

As the leading lady in *Titanic*, the most popular movie in the history of film, Kate Winslet has been both adored as a sex symbol and disparaged as overweight. The British actress has consistently spoken out against what she sees as abnormal expectations among American viewers and the Hollywood hotshots who control celebrities' careers.

Winslet recounts struggling with her weight as a child, slimming down through the Weight Watchers program, and then taking her weight-loss objective too far. She has credited one of her costars with steering her in the right direction. "When I was making *Sense and Sensibility,* Emma Thompson noticed that I'd skip lunch and not eat properly," Kate told Australia's *Who* magazine. "She said, 'If you dare try and lose weight for this job, I will be furious with you.' She went out and bought me *The Beauty Myth* [by Naomi Wolf], and since then, I've been much more relaxed about that side of it."

"I really have been to hell and back with this whole blooming weight thing," Kate told interviewer Clive James on the British *Clive James Show.* "I was very big when I was younger and very sensibly lost a lot of weight and then went the other way and made myself really quite ill, and now I'm reaching the point where I'm happy." Kate hopes her experience can send a message to young girls today. "I'm not a model, I'm an actress. . . . It's quite a nice feeling to know that I'm in *Titanic* and I'm playing one of the leading roles and I am not the waiflike norm you would see in Hollywood. And it's quite important to me that I stand there as a British woman and say, 'Listen girls out there, don't go starving yourselves 'cause there's just no point.'"

that all of your progress will be wasted if you take a week off. If you suffer an injury, find ways to exercise without using that part of your body. For example, if you hurt your knee, come up with a set of seated exercises to keep your arms and your other leg in shape. If you break your wrist, you can still walk or run. It's a good idea to think ahead and plan how you will vary your routine if you catch a cold or hurt yourself; that way you'll be prepared to step right into plan B when the time comes. It is also smart to study ways to prevent injuries linked to overexertion, including muscle strains, sprains, and stress fractures, and how to treat them if they do occur.

⊙ If you exercise outdoors, always keep your personal safety in mind. Always carry identification, even if you're only going around the block. If you wear headphones, know that you might not hear someone coming up behind you or a car headed your way. When walking or jogging, especially at night, carry a whistle, a can of pepper spray, a cell phone, or some other item to help you if you are confronted by a mugger. Note that pepper spray can help you fend off an attacking dog as well, and a cell phone will become your most prized possession if you injure yourself and can't get home on your own. If you bike or in-line skate, always wear a helmet—no excuses!

⊙ Prepare to change your exercise routine when you reach your goal weight. After reading about how eating disorders start, you know that it is important to know when to ease up on your exercising, so think about it now. You might plan to switch to exercising every other day, or to try a new sport or activity to maintain your weight and fitness level without overdoing it.

FINALLY, IF YOU REMEMBER JUST ONE THING...

Remember that you are doing this for yourself, not for your friends' approval or to finally get that dream date. Once you reach your goals, you will still be the same person—being at your ideal weight will not make you any better than anyone else, just as being at a less than ideal level did not make you any worse than anyone else. Improving your nutritional habits and fitness level will improve your overall health, and as a result you will probably look better by society's standards, but never forget that your physical appearance has nothing to do with your value as a person.

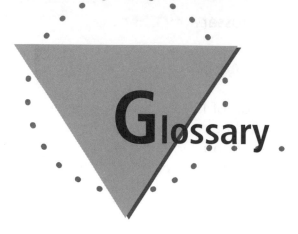

Glossary

alcoholism   Psychological and nutritional disease characterized by an inability to resist alcoholic drinks.

amenorrhea   Cessation of normal menstrual periods; sometimes caused by excessive weight loss.

antidepressant   Drug designed to relieve feelings of depression.

cardiovascular   Relating to the heart and blood vessels.

diuretic   Drug that increases the flow of urine.

empathy   The ability to be aware of and sensitive to the unspoken thoughts and feelings of another person.

logo (short for logotype)   An identifying mark used by commercial firms for advertising purposes.

malnutrition   State of being inadequately nourished, either because of poverty or excessive dieting.

obsession   Unwanted preoccupation with an idea
  or an action.
osteoporosis   Condition of loss of bone mass,
  leading to fragility and ease of fracture.
pathogenic   Capable of causing disease.
promotion   Actions designed to further the acceptance and sale of goods through advertising or
  price discounting.

Where to Go for Help

American Anorexia/Bulimia Association, Inc.
(AABA)
165 West 46th Street, Suite 1108
New York, NY 10036
(212) 575-6200
Web site: http://www.aabainc.org
Committed to increasing public awareness of eating disorders and providing treatment information and referrals to sufferers and their families and friends.

Anorexia Nervosa and Bulimia Association (ANBA)
767 Bayridge Drive
P.O. Box 20058
Kingston, Ontario
K7P1C0
(613) 547-3584
Web site: http://www.ams.queensu.ca/anab
Canadian organization with twenty-four-hour crisis and information hotline.

Anorexia Nervosa and Related Eating Disorders,
      Inc. (ANRED)
P.O. Box 5102
Eugene, OR 97405
(541) 344-1144
Web site: http://www.anred.com

Center for the Study of Anorexia and Bulimia
1841 Broadway, 4th Floor
New York, NY 10023
(212) 595-3449

Eating Disorders Awareness and Prevention (EDAP)
603 Stewart Street, Suite 803
Seattle, WA 98101
(206) 382-3587
Web site: http://members.aol.com/edapinc
Dedicated to increasing the awareness and prevention of eating disorders. Sponsor of National
Eating Disorders Awareness Week every February;
provides assistance in organizing local events and
educational programs.

National Association of Anorexia Nervosa and
      Associated Disorders (ANAD)
P.O. Box 7
Highland Park, IL 60035
(847) 831-3438

National Eating Disorders Organization (NEDO)
6655 South Yale Avenue
Tulsa, OK 74316
(918) 481-4044

Web site:
http:www.laureate.com/nedonedointro.asap
Provides information on anorexia, bulimia, and binge-eating disorder and on recovery and treatment.

Rader Programs
(800) 841-1515
Web site: http://www.raderpro.com
Offers eating disorder treatment programs in California, Illinois, and Oklahoma.

The Renfrew Center
(800) RENFREW (800-736-3739)
Web site: http://www.renfrew.org
Provides information on its treatment centers in the U.S. as well as general information and referrals.

S.A.F.E. (Self Abuse Finally Ends)
(800) DON'T-CUT (800-366-8288)
7115 West North Avenue
Suite 319
Oak Park, IL 60302
Dedicated to reducing the burden of suffering caused by self-abuse. Provides information, support, and treatment programs for victims.

S.A.F.E. in Canada
735 Wonderland Road North
London, Ontario
N6H5N7
(519) 857-7259

HOT LINES:

(800) THERAPIST Network
(800) 843-7274
Provides referrals to local therapists for any condition.

Boys Town USA
(800) 448-3000
Hearing Impaired: (800) 448-1833
Twenty-four-hour crisis line for all children—girls
and boys—who need help with any problem.
Parents are also welcome to call. Spanish-speak-
ing counselors and translation service for many
other languages available.

Bulimia and Self-Help Hotline
(314) 588-1683
A twenty-four-hour crisis line.

**National Mental Health Association Information
        Center**
(800) 969 NMHA (800-969-6642)
Provides referrals to local Mental Health
Association offices, which can refer you to local
programs.

For or Further Reading

Andersen, Arnold E. *Males with Eating Disorders.* Philadelphia, PA: Brunner/Mazel, 1990.

Barr, Linda. *Emily's Secret: No One Can Find Out* (fiction). St. Petersburg, FL: Willowisp Press/Pages Press, 1997.

Bode, Janet. *Food Fight: A Guide to Eating Disorders for Preteens and Their Parents.* New York: Simon & Schuster, 1997.

Cooper, Peter J. *Bulimia Nervosa & Binge-Eating: A Guide to Recovery.* New York: New York University Press, 1995.

Davis, Brangien. *What's Real, What's Ideal: Overcoming a Negative Body Image.* New York: Rosen Publishing Group, 1999.

Duker, Marilyn, and Roger Slade. *Anorexia Nervosa and Bulimia: How to Help.* Bristol, PA: Open University Press, 1988.

Hall, Lindsey, and Leigh Cohn. *Bulimia: A Guide to Recovery.* Carlsbad, CA: Gurze Designs&Books, 1992.

Hall, Liza F. *Perk! The Story of a Teenager with Bulimia.* Carlsbad, CA: Gurze Designs&Books, 1997.

For Further Reading

Harmon, Dan, and Carol C. Nadelson. *Anorexia Nervosa: Starving for Attention*. Broomball, PA: Chelsea House, 1998.

Hollis, Judi. *Fat Is a Family Affair: A Guide for People with Eating Disorders and Those Who Love Them*. Center City, MN: Hazelden, 1996.

Katherine, Anne. *Anatomy of a Food Addiction: The Brain Chemistry of Overeating*. Carlsbad, CA: Gurze Designs&Books, 1997.

Kolodny, Nancy J. *When Food's a Foe: How You Can Confront and Conquer Your Eating Disorder*. New York: Little, Brown & Co., 1998.

Levine, Michael. *How Schools Can Help Combat Student Eating Disorders: Anorexia Nervosa and Bulimia*. Washington, DC: NEA Professional Library, 1987.

Newman, Leslea. *Fat Chance* (fiction). New York: Paper Star, 1996.

Pipher, Mary. *Reviving Ophelia: Saving the Selves of Adolescent Girls*. New York: Ballantine Books, 1995.

Poulton, Terry. *No Fat Chicks: How Big Business Profits by Making Women Hate Their Bodies—and How to Fight Back*. Secaucus, NJ: Birch Lane Press, 1997.

Prussin, Rebecca, Philip Harvey, and Theresa Foy Digeronimo. *Hooked on Exercise: How to Understand and Manage Exercise Addiction*. New York: Fireside, 1992.

Rowland, Cynthia Joye. *The Monster Within: Overcoming Bulimia*. Grand Rapids, MI: Spirit Press, 1998.

Sandbeck, Terence J. *The Deadly Diet: Recovering from Anorexia and Bulimia*. Oakland, CA: New Harbinger Publications, 1993.

Sheppard, Kay. *Food Addiction: The Body Knows*. Deerfield Beach, FL: Health Communications, 1993.

Sherman, Roberta Trattner, and Ron A. Thompson. *Bulimia: A Guide for Family & Friends.* San Francisco: Jossey-Bass Publishers, 1997.

Siegel, Michele, Judith Brisman, and Margot Weinshel. *Surviving an Eating Disorder: New Perspectives and Strategies for Families and Friends.* New York: HarperCollins, 1997.

Wolf, Naomi. *The Beauty Myth: How Images of Beauty Are Used Against Women.* New York: Anchor, 1992.

WEB SITES:

American Psychiatric Association On line. "Eating Disorders."
http://www.psycho.org/public_info/eating.html
Provides information on anorexia and bulimia, including an extensive section on their possible causes.

Elliott, K.D. "BED Confessions."
http://www.bewell.com/healthy/man/1998/bed
Contains information on binge-eating disorder (BED)

Kansas State University Counseling Services. "Eating Disorders: Bulimia."
http://www.ksu.edu/ucs/bulimia.html
Contains many self-help suggestions.

Knowlton, Leslie. "Eating Disorders in Males."
http://www.mhsource.com/edu/psytimes/p950942.html
Discussion of the impact of anorexia and bulimia on male sufferers.

Larsen, Joanne. "Ask the Dietitian."
http://www.dietitian.com/bulimia.html
Contains questions about bulimia and answers from the doctor.

Mudgett, Heather. "Eating Disorders."
http://www.suite101/article.cfm/eating_disorders/9979
Contains information and links on famous eating-disorder victims.

The Something Fishy Website on Eating Disorders.
http://www.something-fishy.org
Huge collection of information, true stories, help sources, music, remembrances of deceased sufferers, links, and empowering support. Sponsors live chat events with guests whose lives have been impacted by eating disorders.

University of Minnesota Duluth Counseling Services.
    "Eating Disorders"
http://www.dumn.edu/hlthserv/counseling/eating_disor-
    der.html
A scored checklist to evaluate yourself for an eating disorder.

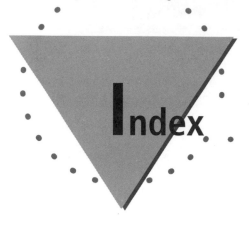

Index